Parenting the Screenager

Richard Hogan

Parenting the Screenager

A Practical Guide for Parents of the Modern Child

Richard Hogan

Published by

Orpen Press
Upper Floor, Unit K9
Greenogue Business Park
Rathcoole
Co. Dublin
Ireland

email: info@orpenpress.com
www.orpenpress.com

© Richard Hogan, 2020

Paperback ISBN 978-1-78605-083-0
ePub ISBN 978-1-78605-084-7

A catalogue record for this book is available from the British Library. All rights reserved. No part of this publication may be reproduced, stored in a retrieval system or transmitted in any form or by any means, electronic, mechanical, photocopying, recording or otherwise, without the prior, written permission of the publisher.

This book is sold subject to the condition that it shall not, by way of trade or otherwise, be lent, resold, hired out, or otherwise circulated without the publisher's prior consent in any form of binding or cover other than that in which it is published and without a similar condition including this condition being imposed on the subsequent purchaser.

This book is designed to provide information and support to our readers. It is not intended as a substitute for professional advice from mental health or childcare professionals. The reader should always consult a relevant professional when required. The content of this book is the sole expression and opinion of the author. No warranties or guarantees are expressed or implied by the publisher's choice to include any of the content in this volume. Neither the publisher nor the author shall be liable for any physical, psychological, emotional, financial or commercial damages, including, but not limited to, special, incidental, consequential or other damages.

Printed in Dublin by SPRINTprint Ltd

To my mother, you were always there in the cold winter evenings to collect us. You taught me about love and fun.

Acknowledgements

To my wife, Erica; your support throughout this book has remained the one constant driving force. You have always been the light that guides me. To my three daughters, Hannah, Lizzy and Sophie. Nothing I have read in a book or theory I have studied in university ever taught me how to be a good father like you three girls. You give my life meaning. To my grandmother, your sense of humour is always with me.

I would like to acknowledge the work of my editor, Eileen O'Brien, whose clear eye kept this book on point.

I also owe a debt of gratitude to Esther McCarthy, who took a gamble and gave me my own column with the *Irish Examiner*. Her unrelenting Cork wit makes sure I never take myself too seriously. And to Darren Mahon, thank you for bringing my vision of Therapy Institute to life.

'What will survive of us is love', Philip Larkin.

Contents

Foreword	viii
Introduction	1
1. Boundaries	3
2. The Dawn of the Screenager	18
3. Building Levels of Communication with a Screenager	37
4. Approaches to Gaming	43
5. Online Pornography	56
6. Bullying	68
7. Cyberbullying	76
8. Modern Approaches to Teenage Anxiety	85
9. Perfectionism, Body Image and Steroid Use	112
10. Sleep Deprivation and Exams	119
11. The Modern Family	124
12. Conclusion	132

Foreword

Richard Hogan's timely book is written for anyone looking for practical parenting assistance in a rapidly changing world. This is a book designed to help parents or carers guide their children through the maze of their increasingly complex teenage years. Few would argue that the lives of young people are simpler now that before. One only needs to consider the pervasiveness of smartphone technology, the rise of social media and the increasing prevalence of mental health issues. It can be tough to know how to really connect with your screenager.

As a family therapist I hear parents discuss the difficulty in keeping up with the speed of change in their children's lives. And yet, this parental concern provides an insight into the world that young people inhabit. A world that often not only appears unfamiliar but at times seems frankly unknowable.

A world where a sixteen-year-old girl recently told me that she just had to bring two large suitcases away for a two-night hotel stay with her mum. She could not understand 'what the big deal was' for her mum regarding such volume of luggage. One suitcase was full of clothes for everyday wear and the other was for her to dress for her Instagram photos. She informed me that 'I could not be seen dead in the same clothes!'

Foreword

Or the young man who commented on how a chap he ignores in real life is a friend on Facebook. This relationship is one limited to conversing with each other online. When I enquired how this worked in real time he said, 'ah if we bump into each other on the street, we just walk right by as if we don't know each other, and then chat online afterwards.' If this world of the screenager is one you are playing catch-up with, take heart. *Parenting the Screenager* will not only point you in the right direction, it will help equip you for the twists and turns that lie ahead.

In clinical practice I have worked with thousands of parents during the past twenty years. Increasingly during the past few years many have described a feeling of disorientation – doing their best, but at times holding on by their fingertips. If this strikes a chord the practical ideas introduced in this book will alleviate some of your concerns.

How then can the curious parent even begin to make sense of their role in all of this? Even with the best of parenting intentions it can be so difficult when an issue arises to know how to engage young people without unwittingly pushing them further away. Welcome to the law of unintended consequences, where the opposite effect of your good intentions is achieved.

How can a modern parent hold a balance between helping their teen or young adult to build resilience and not overplay all the potential hazards that await them? Unwittingly, many young people have been sold a pernicious lie. That life runs in straight lines. As adults we know it never does and those who expect it to are being set up to be let down!

It's an irony in life that those who insist in trying to help us often end up harming us the most. For instance, please recall an over-jealous parent who tried to split up 'young love' only to find that the opposite effect was achieved – the young lovers driven into a deeper embrace. How is it that our well-intentioned 'help' often ends up hindering?

Despite the bad rap that screenagers often get, this is just one side of the coin. Even for a teen who is testing your parental capacity to the limit, there is much to admire if you learn how to look. Developing that skill is priceless. Many times a screenager's protestations arise from idealism, which you may feel life needs to take the rough edges off.

One ought to remember though, that it is not your job as a parent to shoehorn anyone into your desires for what you feel 'is best for them'. It is their life and theirs to direct as they choose. It is incumbent on us to help screenagers to find the direction for the path they are called to tread.

I have noticed that parents who breeze through the trials of life (well most of them anyway) usually have one thing in common. They don't just love their children, they make a point in also liking them. This may seem a little odd, allow me to explain. You might have heard a parent talking about how they would take a bullet for their child, in other words die for them. How noble. Who could argue with this? Allow me. I believe that dying for a cause is much easier than living for one. If we really love our children, they will be under no doubt that we also like them. Not merely humouring them or reminding them of all the things we do for them. If you think that young people can't read between these lines be assured from someone who has spoken to thousands of them that they can, and they do.

Put your hand on your heart and ask yourself the following, if I was my son or daughter would I be under no doubt whatsoever that I really like them in addition to loving them? What would be the proof they would find? Do I demonstrate a capacity to mercilessly listen to what my screenager says even if I don't like hearing it, before wading in with my vast expertise? Do I spend time with that teen or child one-to-one, because the relationship is important enough to prioritise, even with the busyness of modern life? This is just a little of the feedback from many conversations I have had with frustrated screenagers having to manage their parents' challenging behaviour.

And finally, a friend of mine told me about a bird that builds a nest which is lined by lovely soft downy feathers. Before the feathers are laid, thorns are used to line the nest. When the chick is hatched, all it feels is the lovely soft feathers. Over time as the bird grows it pushes down more and more on the feathers and little by little the thorns push their way through. As the bird grows bigger and bigger it feels sufficiently discomforted to eventually leave the nest.

As a metaphor for parenting, I have come across none better than the conditions created in this bird's nest. The challenge for all parents

Foreword

is to find a way to hold in mind both the comfort and growth of their offspring. If they exclusively prioritise the child's comfort do you really think they will ever voluntarily leave the nest? On the other hand, if the child is pushed out too soon they will not have developed the requisite abilities to survive flying the coop, and if they do leave, will find a way to keep returning battered and bruised.

Remember young people are shrewd. Their BS detector is seriously attuned. They know if you are going through the motions or if your heart is really in it. Now here is an apparently bonkers sounding idea which I can guarantee works. If parenting at times feels like trying to push an elephant uphill, the thing to do is to act like you are gently guiding a slightly wayward fluffy kitten. Believe it or not, like an alchemist, little by little, you will eventually change the elephant into a kitten.

Shake out of your system any parenting ideas that are not working. Try something different, such as the ideas that Richard will introduce you to. Laugh at yourself more. As a wise person once said, 'some issues are too important to be taken seriously.' Do what needs to be done, but with a kind heart. Allow your creativity to expand you; even if you are not in the habit of doing so, please begin. If you tell yourself you are creative and look hard enough you will find the evidence to confirm this.

A final word to the wise. Practice what you preach when it comes to screen use. If you meet your screenager halfway, I have found that they will gladly meet you in the middle.

Don Boardman, family therapist

Introduction

In my experience working clinically as a psychotherapist, principal, schoolteacher and lecturer I have been struck by the sheer number of students needing help navigating the modern world. Parents are finding it increasingly difficult to know what to do with the young teenager or adult in the house struggling with a mental health issue. The nature of the modern family has changed too. Couples are generally meeting later in life and therefore are subsequently having children at a later stage, so parents are often that little bit older having a teenager in the house. And the world of the teenager has dramatically changed over the previous number of years. I believe it is like no other time that has gone before. The gap between the adult world and the teenage world is striking, and it places considerable pressure on the family as a unit. The arrival of ubiquitous internet and the proliferation of technology means that new vistas and ways of communicating are possible. Communication has significantly changed over the last fifteen years. The nature of modern communication among teenagers is different too; it is more abbreviated, instantaneous and functional, so parents often find themselves struggling to open up the lines of communication with their child. However, it is important to understand that communication is not the same as when we were young. We have to now learn how to engage with our teenager in a new way that promotes a healthy and happy home life for everyone in that ecology.

This book is a practical guide to help parents build levels of communication in the family. It will utilise case studies from my clinical practice and will outline different parental strategies and approaches to help parents become more effective in their parenting. There is no doubt about it, parenting well-adjusted children in the modern world is more difficult than at any other time before. Both parents are generally working to meet the financial demands that this modern world places on us and this means that they often do not see their child as much as they would like. This can impact considerably on how they parent their child. This book will discuss modern approaches to modern parenting; it will provide you with new ideas on how to parent your child. And it will give you clear strategies for dealing with issues that I have seen again and again in my work as a systemic family psychotherapist.

1

Boundaries

I am starting this book with a chapter on boundaries because all of what follows is really built on the premise that a child needs clear and concise boundaries. As parents, we must be the ones who teach our children the dos and don'ts of navigating the family unit and wider society as a whole. However, the kind of boundaries I'm speaking of here are boundaries that are supportive and do not annihilate the spirit of the child. Boundaries are what keep a child safe; in my experience children often test the boundaries to see if in fact they are being held and whether or not they are safe in that system. We must be consistent when we are setting boundaries for our children. Nothing promotes negative behaviour more than inconsistent parenting. As parents, we must ask ourselves:

- Why are we inconsistent?
- Why is one parent more permissive than the other?
- Could I be parenting from a position of guilt?
- Whose needs do I meet when I renege on a promised punishment?

These are important questions to consider when you are examining your child's negative behaviour and I will explore each of these questions in this chapter. In my experience, I meet many parents who access my service when their child is in their late teens and they are finding it almost impossible to control them. In those early conversations I explore the notion of boundaries and in nearly all cases where the child is dictating the rules in the house, permissive parenting styles have been present from a very early age. I had one mother recently tell me about her negative relationship with her son. She said that 'he decides when he comes home' when I asked her how her son leaves the house and regarding the instructions he receives, she told me, 'I tell him not to be late'. When I inquired what being late meant for her she said, 'oh, I don't really know; before 1 or 2 a.m.' And when I spoke with her son and asked him what would he do if he was told to be in for 10 p.m., he told me, 'I wouldn't put up with that.' I asked him what happens when he is late; unsurprisingly he responded 'nothing'. It was obvious from these early conversations that the child had received a very clear message that consequences and ramifications for breaking boundaries were non-existent in the family, so he had learned that he could dictate his own rules for being in the family. I see this kind of behaviour more and more. The behaviour of the child becomes so uncontrollable that parents suddenly begin to realise that there is a major issue and they finally try to set boundaries but the behaviour is firmly entrenched, so these boundaries create huge conflict and distress in the family. Parents often seek help after a major blow-up has occurred in the family. And of course, all habits and behaviours can be broken and corrected but it is far more difficult to break a behaviour that is entrenched than one that is forming. So, setting clear boundaries early on in the family are very important for the future happiness and contentment of that family unit. Your child will thank you for it later in their life when they are capable of experiencing joy and happiness and also when they have the skills and resilience to cope with those difficult moments which will inevitably occur.

When a child receives the message in their formative years that the world will shape itself around them to suit their needs they are being set up for a very unhappy adult life. We all know the type of child I'm referring to. The one who cannot share, the one who has no joy on their birthday because it wasn't exactly how they wanted it to be. The kind of child who has an expectancy of others and refuses to offer their own time for anything. I'm not just talking about a spoilt child here; I'm referring to a child who lacks the capacity for joy. Their parents have implicitly told them that their every whim will be satiated and therefore they have come to expect it. But they have done them such a disservice; they have made it nearly impossible for that child to experience happiness in their adult life because, as we all know, the adult world does not work like that. The fall they get when they are forced to confront that reality can be devastating to their psyche. The child who gets everything appreciates nothing. The partners whom these types of children marry have to 're-parent' them in that relationship, because being a spoilt adult isn't conducive to a functioning family unit. And they are impossible to live with because they believe everything must shape around them, so when they have children the conflict is massively heightened because they have never learned to compromise or face a challenge. And let's face it, having children and rearing them successfully and being a functioning member of your relationship is incredibly challenging and if you fundamentally believe that the world owes you happiness you will be bitterly disappointed when you find out the truth. I see these types of adult males a lot in my practice. They nearly all have the same characteristics: stubborn, reticent, quick-tempered, and unmoving in their position. I hear the wife describing her experience in the house living with a man who refuses to carry his weight in the relationship. What is striking about this type of adult male is that in nearly all of the cases I have worked with the male partner cannot hear his partner's position and I often wonder is it that they are not able to hear it because they have been told from such a young age that they do not need to meet any one's demands or expectations. It is such a damaging mindset to teach your child. And, ultimately, the paradox is in your bid to make your child happy all the time you are actually creating the scenario where your child will never be happy in later life. Your job as a parent is to launch healthy children into the world. And if you parent them in a way that gives them unrealistic expectations of the world you are setting them up for a fall. You are also setting yourself up for a very uncomfortable and conflict-filled number of years because they will live in your house as they want or as you told them they can. So building boundaries that do not collapse the moment they are tested is crucial to your child's happiness. And, as I said, they will thank you for setting clear boundaries later in life when they are highly functioning and happy in the world and have the capacity to compromise.

Types of Boundaries

Setting healthy, clear boundaries that respect the individuality of your child is crucial for a successful, happy home. I often meet families where the boundaries are in place but they are stifling the spirit of the child. Boundaries must never be destructive; they are meant to be supportive. They are in place to help your child navigate the world and to understand that there are consequences for their behaviours. The ultimate goal of a clear, healthy boundary that respects the child is to help the child understand how to make the right decision when you are not looking. When we think about slapping as a response to a boundary being broken we can see why boundaries are important. Let's just say you come home from a long day and your child is playing the computer, you ask them to stop and they don't. You're tired and you've being working all day and your child is pushing your competencies and patience. So you grab the game and slap them and tell them never to be cheeky to you again. What has been achieved here? Well, many things. Your child knows now never to play the game before you come in, because you are likely to be tired, hungry and aggressive and you will hurt them if you catch them playing the game. They also learn how to be deceptive. They are not going to get caught again! Going forward in their life, they will develop this response to avoid getting caught in any behaviour they feel may not be well received. But what have they learned that is positive for their life? Nothing. All they've learned is not to get caught because Mum or Dad will overreact. And that is the complete opposite of why a boundary is in place. Boundaries teach our children how to navigate the world. They teach them to make the right decision when they are alone and free to make a choice that may have negative consequences for their life. Slapping your child teaches them to never get caught. There is a huge difference here for the thought process of your child and for the future happiness of that child as they move into adult life.

Authoritarian Boundaries

'Where there is power, there is resistance' (Michel Foucault)

An authoritarian style of parenting is as destructive to your child's psyche as absolute permissive parenting. They both achieve the same outcome: an unhappy, confused child. I see it so often in my clinical practice – parents seek out therapy for their child who they feel is depressed and in my early conversations the child delineates a stifling environment which they have no understanding of how to navigate successfully. An authoritarian boundary can annihilate the spirit of the child because once they break the boundary they are completely destroyed.

Case Study of Authoritarian Boundaries

John was brought to me because his mother was worried that he seemed withdrawn and down. She was concerned because he had started to lose interest in activities that once brought him joy. In my early conversation with John's mother I felt there was something missing from the conversation. She was a meek lady, quite nervous and very worried about her child. When I asked how her husband fathered John she became a little defensive and explained that he was very strict but that his own father was strict too and that he only wanted the best for John. When I first met

John, I was struck by how quiet and small he made himself for such a big young man. Initially we discussed how he was feeling but it didn't take us long to start looking at the types of messages he was receiving:

Richard: When is your mood at its lowest?
John: When I hear the car.
Richard: The car?
John: When Dad's home.
Richard: Okay, so before Dad comes home what is the house like?
John: Nice.
Richard: And when Dad comes home what changes?
John: Everything. Mum, me, everything.
Richard: Can you describe that more?
John: It's like the air disappears. Mum says Dad can't help it, he was raised that way, but I can never please him. I got an A- in my Maths test and he wanted to know where I lost the marks.
Richard: Is there ever a time you enjoy his company?
John: Sometimes having a kickabout, but that normally ends up with him getting annoyed that I'm not kicking the ball the right way: 'on the side of the foot'. (John mimics his father's austere tone and throws his eyes up in frustration.)
Richard: Can you describe a time you had a fight with Dad?
John: Yeah, nearly every day. Last week, I had finished my homework and I started to play a couple of games of *Fortnite* and he just came home; he looked in and said, 'you should be doing your homework.' When I told him I had done it, he grabbed the game off me and took it away and I haven't seen it since.
Richard: What did Mum say about that?
John: Nothing. She goes along with him. Like last month, we have a rule that I cannot play the PlayStation for more than 40 minutes a day and I stick to it, it's not worth the hassle. But last month Dad burst into my room and said 'you're playing

> more than 40 minutes', it might have been about 41 minutes, and he took the game away for three weeks. I only got it back last week and it's gone again, for what? I can't wait to be old enough to move out and have my own house. I'm sick of it, I can't take it.

Here we can see a young man struggling to navigate a house that is governed by an authoritarian style of parenting. It is restrictive and claustrophobic and is destroying the spirit of the young boy who has to grow up in it. And again we can see how this will stay with the young man long into his adult life. John stayed for a few more sessions but when I talked to his father about parenting approaches the sessions ended. The father couldn't face the fact that perhaps the way he was parenting his child wasn't the most productive and in fact was causing his child such harm. This was how he was parented and nothing was going to stop him from passing it on to his child.

'People know what they do; frequently they know why they do what they do; but what they don't know is what what they do does' (Michel Foucault). I think this quote from the French philosopher sums up this father's position well. And I have met many adults who have been brought up like John and in nearly all cases they have a fractured relationship with their parents and struggle with intimacy issues in their own personal relationships. Your family is not meant to be under your control; you are not the tsar of a small country. You are trying to promote the situation where your child can be a part of and separate from your family. They must go forward into the world as confident, content young adults and an authoritarian approach to parenting ensures that that is impossible.

Permissive Boundaries

As I said above, nothing promotes negative behaviour in children more than inconsistent parenting. Boundaries that do not hold are an exercise in futility. If one parent is more permissive than the other it erodes any potential for your child to learn how to navigate the world. If you are reading this and this resonates with you ask yourself, why is my partner more likely to give into my child's demands than I am? What does this behaviour say about your partner and the way they were raised? Is your partner consumed with being your child's best friend? Discuss this with them. Often we are blind to the motives of our behaviours until someone points them out to us. And often we are permissive because we were raised in an authoritarian house. Think of the case study of John; what type of parent is he likely to make? Will he be authoritarian? Or permissive? It is more likely that he will be permissive; I can imagine him uttering something like, 'no child of mine will ever be told what to do.' And this is often what happens. Because we were oppressed as children we now mistakenly believe that to have a boundary is placing us in the position of an authoritarian despot. And nothing could be further from the truth. It is this misapprehension that causes many parents to adopt a permissive parenting style and this causes so much conflict for them in their lives. And they cannot understand why their child, who has it all, does not respect them like they had to respect their father who treated them very poorly. This is the contradiction of permissive parenting. In your bid to make your child happy you are making everyone in the family unit miserable. A child who receives mixed messages about boundaries will not respect them. And a child who does not respect boundaries will make for a very difficult adolescent and an even more troubled adult. I hear the following phrase nearly every day in my practice: 'where did I go wrong?' And in nearly all cases the absence of clear boundaries is at the root cause of the conflict. Both parents must sit down and have a conversation about the types of boundaries they feel the house should operate under. I call these types of boundaries the non-negotiable ones. For example, the time your child has to come in at: this is a safety issue and should be a non-negotiable boundary. Of course your child will use all sorts of persuasive language to get you to acquiesce on this but you both must be resolute and hold firm together. When one parent is more lenient and gives in on a boundary, they are telling the child that the boundaries do not exist and that all boundaries can be broken. And a house that operates under those kinds of rules is going to have a lot of conflict in it. I will return to inconsistent parenting later in this chapter.

Authoritative Boundaries

Authoritative parenting is the most desirable approach a parent can take when it comes to setting very clear and concise rules for the family system. As a species we respond well to rules that are fair and easy to understand. Every house should have clear and concise boundaries framed in a language that everyone in the unit can understand. There is no point setting out rules in a form of language that a child or teenager does not understand. Keep it simple and relatable. Explain the reason for the boundary and the consequences if that boundary is broken. Remember John's story; when he broke the boundary there was a disproportionate response and that is not healthy. The type of boundary I'm speaking about here is a boundary that holds the child and supports them. It does not annihilate them when they break it, because your child will test the boundaries and they will break them and that is why you must put clear ramifications and consequences in place for that eventuality.

Let's just say you have told your child he can only play three games of *Fortnite* a night during the weeknights and you discover that while you were out he had been playing it for over three hours. In John's case he over-played by a few minutes, his father was waiting to catch him so he could show him who is boss. But a healthy boundary allows for it to be broken. A healthy boundary moves slightly but comes back into place. What I'm speaking of here is a boundary that does not erode your child's sense of self. So you catch your child playing for three hours. What do you do? Well, before you placed the boundary around gaming during the weeknights, hopefully you explained to your child that if they over-game they will lose the privilege of gaming the following night and if they behave they will get the game back the night after but they will only be allowed to play one game a night until they show that they can respect the boundary. When that happens they will be able to play three games a night again. So, the boundary was broken, there was no overreaction, shouting or aggression but rather a calm conversation about the fact that the boundary will come back into place and not change. Of course, your child might get annoyed but you do not meet their annoyance with yours. Model how you cope with tension. Show them that breaking the boundary has consequences and that once they can respect those consequences they will be able to play the game again like you agreed in the first place. In setting clear boundaries we must also set clear consequences. Your child is going to break the boundaries you set, because they are not robots. You do not want to raise robots so when they break the boundary it is crucial that your reaction is measured and without hyperbolic drama. When a boundary is broken it must not mean total annihilation for your child. As the parent, you must teach them why the boundaries are there in the first place; once they understand the logic of the boundary it is easier for them to follow it. For example, when you are setting the gaming boundary you could say something like, 'gaming is addictive, and you cannot play it for as long as you want. Of course you can play your game every day but not all the time. So we've decided you can play three games a night. I know that is about an hour of *Fortnite* so please only play three games. I'll know if you play for longer and if I find that you have been gaming for longer you will lose your gaming privileges the following day and after that you will only be able to play one game a night until we see that you can obey the boundary.' Here you are explaining why you have brought in the boundary and the consequence for breaking it. This is a fair boundary with reasonable consequences and you are also teaching your child how to become self-directed and self-regulated, which really is the goal of setting a boundary in the first place.

How Do I Set Boundaries When My Child Has Never Had to Obey Them Before?

If you have a teenage son/daughter in the house and you have never really had clear and concise boundaries in place and there have been no consequences for that child's behaviour, it's now about rowing back on your parenting approaches. You can't bring in too many boundaries at once. Too much difference is not good for a child. I often meet parents who leave the therapeutic setting wildly enthusiastic about all the boundaries they are going to put in place when they get home. I meet the same parents the following week bitterly disappointed and despondent because the rule changes they tried to implement didn't have any impact on the family. They tried too much, too soon. Remember if you have never had boundaries in place before, pick one that you feel is really important for your family. Say, the boundary around what time your child comes in at — this is one that I feel is a non-negotiable one, because it ensures the safety of your child. You should have a conversation with your partner, or other parents if you are a single parent, and figure out what is a reasonable time to expect your child home at. So, you've decided on 9 p.m. weeknights for your sixteen-year-old. Now, they have never had to obey a boundary before, so this is going to be more difficult to impose, but not impossible. Of course they will fight it, because they have always got their own way. Be prepared for the fight, and don't rise to their bait. They will say things to get you upset in the hope that you will just give in, in annoyance — 'Look, fine; do whatever you want' — that's the kind of reaction they are hoping for when they bait you. But don't allow them to position you like that. Be calm. This is why you only bring in one rule change at a time if your child is not used to them. Make the ramifications something that you can follow through on. The most destructive type of ramifications are the ones that cannot be implemented. For example, if you say something like 'if you're not in by 9 p.m. you're never going out again' your child knows that you can't follow through on that threat, so it has no value. I have often noticed a commonality among families that struggle with boundaries. They generally tend to have issues with language. What I mean by this is that in some families where there are no boundaries the parents over-use exaggerated language to try to put a consequence in place: 'That's it, you're never seeing your friends again' or 'I'm never buying you another treat' or 'That's it young lady, you are never going to a disco again!' Tensions heighten extremely quickly; there is no middle ground. And when you launch threats that cannot be followed through on, you are making your position impossible. Your child will see this and they will have no respect for your consequence because they know it can't be implemented. So be careful of your language and if you use language like I'm describing here, change it. Stop using huge threats because they hold no value. The smaller and more doable the threat the better likelihood your child will heed it. This is very important when you are dealing with a child who is not used to following rules. You cannot implement wholescale changes. Less is more in this situation. It's about teaching your child how to obey one simple rule at a time. Eventually, you will notice how easy it is to bring in a rule because your child will have learned how to follow them.

The Damage of Inconsistent Parenting

We've all been there. Tired, perhaps even exhausted, you've just arrived home from a difficult day out with the kids. You've told your children there is going to be ramifications for the behaviour they displayed in public and now you're home it's time to implement those promises but, as I said, you're tired, even exhausted, and you do nothing. Instead your child is in front of you demanding a chocolate biscuit; you know there is no way they should get one but all you want to do is rest. You need some quiet time, some headspace and you've lost all that earlier impetus for a fight. So you give in. Your child has stopped demanding and for a brief moment there is peace in the house and you can finally rest. But you've lost, and recent research shows that this type of inconsistent parenting can, in fact, be damaging your child's sense of self-worth and even future happiness.

Consistent parenting is the process of setting clear rules and boundaries in a language that children can understand. The reality is, all children crave boundaries. They make them feel safe and help them to make sense of the world. In the formative years children are constantly attempting to decipher the messages they are receiving and what those messages say about the kind of person they are in the world. Recently, coming home from the beach my eldest daughter asked me could they have a treat when they got home. I had just bought them an ice cream; I knew there was no way I was going to give into their demands for more empty calories but I didn't want the argument in the car so I said 'maybe'. I knew it was a non-committal response that I could deal with later. But I glimpsed my four-year-old daughter winking at her older sister and whispering 'maybe means yes'. And she was right. As we made the journey home I started to analyse why she would think that.

And why did she ask me and not my wife? I realised that I often say 'maybe' in my attempt to deal with something later that I don't want to deal with in the immediate present. And my four-year-old has figured that out. Our children are always deciphering what our language and actions mean. So we need to be more consistent in what we say and do. When a child knows the rules and consequences for breaking those rules it actually makes them feel safe. That's not to say they won't test the boundaries, of course they will. But, they need to know that those consequences are non-negotiable. This actually makes children feel secure and helps them to make sense of the world. So, when they receive inconsistent messages, it makes the world unpredictable and scary and can cause confusion and create a sense of chaos in that child's head.

Modern parenting is remarkably different than any time that has gone before. Often I have conversations in my practice with young parents who are riddled with guilt because their own parents are vocally critical of how they are raising their children. But the reality of modern parenting makes consistency more difficult to achieve. Couples are meeting later in life and, in general, are having children at a later stage in their life, and also both parents need to work to meet the financial demands of modern living. So parents need to give themselves a break. It's hard; it's always been hard but today's world with the demands it places on parents raising children means that parents are up against it when it comes to being consistent with their parenting approaches. But it's not impossible and if you sit down with your partner and go through a few of the boundaries you believe your child needs, it will make everyone in the family unit more secure in their role.

Three Tips to Avoid Being an Inconsistent Parent

1. Both parents need to be saying the same thing. If one parent is more permissive than the other this will cause tensions within the family unit, as your children will play you both off each other. So you both have to be resolute on the non-negotiable boundaries you have decided on.

2. Never parent from a position of guilt. Just because you work long days and you currently do not see your child as much as you would like, this does not mean that you over-compensate by giving into your child's every whim when you are with them. You are diminishing your role as parent and you are doing your child a disservice.
3. You must always follow through with the consequences. Nothing is more detrimental to creating a happy structured balance in the house than reneging on a promised punishment. When you do this you are telling your child that you are not someone to be trusted and your word means nothing.

Inconsistency in parenting can be easily changed. It takes a conversation with your partner about the clear boundaries you want established in the house and what punishments you feel should be implemented if those boundaries are crossed. You certainly do not want to bring in an authoritarian style of parenting but rather a reasonable and clear set of rules that your child can understand and follow. This will make family life for more rewarding for everyone.

* * *

I started this book exploring the nature of boundaries because I firmly believe that a happy, well-adjusted child is the product of clear and concise boundaries. The messages we receive in childhood are so important for the type of adult we become. In my experience, working with families for many years, it is the absence of boundaries that cause so much of the conflict within a family unit. I have yet to meet an adult who said, 'I really must thank my parents for showing me that my behaviours have no consequences.' You must examine what it is that is holding you back from bringing supportive boundaries into your family. Remember this key phrase: *'be by your child's side, not on it.'* This simple phrase is teaching us that we must never lose sight of our responsibility for the children we have brought into this world. We are not simply our child's best friend or indeed their master; we are the ones in charge of their formation. And we have their future happiness in our hands; it is such an important job rearing a child. We must never lose sight of the task in our eagerness to be liked by our child. Of course I want my children to love me. But I can handle it when they say they don't because I've taken away their favourite toy after a tantrum. Your children will say hurtful things to you over the course of this wonderful and challenging journey together. But see those hurtful words for what they are – their privilege talking. Try to think of the behaviour as the problem, not the child. Try to say something like 'I really didn't like that behaviour; where did that come from?' So you are removing the problem from the child. I have found this very positive with my own children. My seven-year-old daughter said to me recently, 'do you still love me when I'm being bold?' I told her, 'of course I do, I'll always love you. But it's just that behaviour I don't like, and I know you don't like it either – so when it pops up try to stop it from getting you in trouble.' I could see the visible excitement dancing in her eyes because she knew my love wasn't conditional and she was also charged with stopping the behaviour from getting her in trouble. So the problem is the problem, not the child. This theory comes from an Australian family therapist, Michael White, one of the pioneers of narrative therapy. Narrative therapy is interested in how we story our life and how, at times, we struggle with how others place labels on us. I often use narrative therapy strategies when working with adolescents because they really respond to the freeing of labels and narratives. Think about your own child: do you speak about them in concretes? Remember a label doesn't predict the future, it writes it. I've noticed the student who gets labelled as 'lazy' or 'weak' early in their academic career struggles to free themselves from that label and in fact will play up to the label they have been given. If you tell a child they are 'bold' or 'bad', how will they think about themselves? But if you change that message and tell them that the behaviour is negative, not them, you will give them a new way of thinking about their behaviour and the power they have over it.

I believe that if you implement the types of boundaries I am describing here and become more consistent in your parenting approaches, you will notice a remarkable shift in your family dynamic.

2

The Dawn of the Screenager

Not since the 1960s has there been such a glaring gap between the world of the adolescent and the world of the parent. The teenager of the 60s dared do something that had not been done before – they spoke about their feelings and they commented on the nature of the world and the systems they were living in. They critiqued hierarchies and organised themselves collectively against what they saw as tyrannies. This was a very different landscape from the teenage world of their parents, who were expected to be silent and not heard. But 'The Times Were', as Dylan prophetically told us, 'a-Changin''. The teenager of the 60s was born around the end of the Second World War. The teenager of today was born around the arrival and rapid dissemination of digital technology or the Tech War. Understanding this new teenager is vital in developing a successful approach to parenting them.

In a two-part series of academic articles,* Marc Prensky employs an analogy of native speakers and immigrants to describe the generation gap separating adolescents (digital natives) from their parents and teachers (the digital immigrants). The digital natives, Prensky describes, are surrounded by digital media to such an extent that their very brain structures may be different from those of previous generations. The modern teenager is navigating a world where there is a monstrous aperture between them and their parents. The tectonic plates under which the world of the teenager stood has dramatically shifted. Proliferation of technology, exposure to the internet, elaborate use of social media and extensive reliance on various digital devices have all impacted on how they live their lives and how they go about the business of socialising. For example, digital natives are used to receiving information really fast. They like to parallel process and multitask. They prefer their graphics before their text rather than the opposite. They prefer random access (like hypertext). They prefer games to 'serious' work. In contrast, those not born in the digital world, according to Prensky, find it hard to understand how a digital native thinks. This new way of communicating that the digital age has brought with it has interrupted communication patterns. Communication is now abbreviated, fast, instantaneous and functional. What I have often found talking with parents about their child is that they cannot understand why their child refuses to engage with them at the dinner table. And when I talk with the young adolescent about their parents' concern they generally delineate how their parents misinterpret their reticence as some sort of mental dysphoria. 'I have nothing to tell them; nothing happened today in school, so what? Should I just make it up? Is that what they want?' I have heard this sentiment many times in relation to dinnertime conversation, or as one student called it, 'dinnertime interrogation'. And often when we are finding resistance to our questions, maybe it is the questions that are to blame. Maybe we are asking the wrong questions; maybe we are not engaging our children in conversations they are interested in. That is not to say we design

---

* Prensky, Marc (2009) 'H. Sapiens Digital: From Digital Immigrants and Digital Natives to Digital Wisdom', *Innovate: Journal of Online Education*, 5(3).

every question to suit their interests, but if we are getting nowhere maybe we have to rethink how we go about trying to connect with our child.

I have observed over recent years how adolescents even find watching a movie problematic, because it requires a certain level of concentration over a relatively long period of time. Relative, that is, to the modern adolescent. For example, ads on YouTube are five seconds in length – even this is seen as too long. Snapchat conversations are under five seconds in length and they disappear after being read. Until recently, a tweet had to be less than 140 characters; it's now 280 characters. Everything in the adolescent world is quick and multifaceted, so conversations over dinner can seem laborious and unstimulating. Does that mean we give up trying to talk with them? Of course not. But, it is important to know that communication has changed. And when I am talking with an adolescent around their low mood or conflict in the family this idea is certainly present in my questions. I explore communication patterns with their family and friends. And I look at their peer relationships. What I have found is that young adolescents, and in particular young male adolescents, find it difficult to voice a rupture in peer relations. Parents perceive that there is a change in their child but cannot understand what the cause of this change is.

I had a conversation with a parent recently where she described her concerns about her son who had become quite depressed in recent months. She outlined how his mood had changed and the worry herself and her husband were experiencing. In the first few sessions with her son we talked about his mood and how it had changed. However, it wasn't until I looked at his social network that the real issue emerged. He became quite upset when we were looking at his network of friends. One friend in particular caused him great upset. He told me 'take her off the list – she's no friend of mine!' When we explored this further he revealed that he had sent her a compromising picture of himself on Snapchat and she had screenshot it and had sent it to her friends, and now he was the source of derision. And this was causing him much distress. But he couldn't voice this to his parents because he was too embarrassed to tell them and he thought that they would be disappointed in him.

I was very struck by how isolated this young man had become due to this event. The parents were concerned about their child, but had no sense of what the issue was. How could they? They explained to me at great length that they didn't understand anything about technology. So, when they observed their child's emotional decline they had no insight into a potential cause. And as parents we must always be thinking about the different facets of our child's life. The sheer isolation this boy felt was very worrying. In one conversation he told me, through tears, that he had contemplated taking his own life. His story is not uncommon, and unfortunately many families have been left devastated after their child has taken such a drastic action to end an immediate problem. Thankfully on this occasion he did talk to his parents about what was troubling him and the issue was resolved.

Thinking in terms of your child's social network and possible ruptures in that grouping is often very helpful in eliciting important information about what is going on for your child. The arrival of technology means that our children have more public platforms to experience negative interactions with their peer group. There have been huge problems in schools over this issue. Children have found themselves excluded from gaming groups and have had awful things written about them on permanent websites. This can be incredibly isolating for a child to experience and, as parents, we must always be vigilant about what is happening in their digital world.

Life for the modern teenager is remarkably different from any other time that has gone before. Couples are generally marrying later in life and for the most part are subsequently having children at a later stage, which further increases the age gap between parent and child and makes keeping up with all these advances in technology more difficult to stay on top of, but not impossible. And it is our responsibility as parents to manage how our children navigate the world of technology.

The Screenager Arrives

Nothing has invaded our personal worlds with such muted insidiousness than that of our technological devices. One of the most striking features of our society today is the fact that nearly everyone seems to be plugged out of life and plugged into some sort of device as they go about their daily odyssey to work or school. It is something I encounter on my own commute into the city – adults and teenagers alike, head down, feverishly zombie-scrolling through the minutia of the latest post or tweet or whatever it is that is capturing their attention so completely. However, while this may seem like a harmless way to while away those awkward moments on public transport, recent research reveals the harsh reality: we are becoming more and more addicted to our devices. I think it is one of the great sad ironies of this technological revolution: the very thing that was designed to link us all is in fact making us more anxious and isolated. Why is it more and more teenagers are experiencing anxiety and depression? Well, you could argue that teenagers of previous generations didn't have the platform to express their feelings like children of today. You might also argue that technology, in its bid to make life easier and carefree, has in fact invented something that actually has the opposite outcome. Like the agricultural revolution, the technological one has brought us into a way of living we have fully embraced without weighing up the negative impact it is having on us as a people. And I see it more and more in my practice – adolescents coming in because they have such deep feelings of loneliness and isolation. They don't feel a part of anything. They lack that human interaction we all crave as children. I see the manifestations of this on my daily commute: teenagers all sitting together but in fact miles apart, scrolling through their phones silently sharing images. I don't want to technology-bash here, because there are a lot of positives with technology. We are living longer and defeating many of the sizable tools the grim reaper has at his disposal. We are journeying further into our universe, gaining great insights into the nature of how it was formed, to mention a few – so there are many benefits to technology and of course as a species we cannot stand still, for to do so would mean our rapid destruction. But we have to be cognisant of what it is taking from us too, and it's considerable. And, as parents, we need to manage our children's relationship with technology because they are struggling to manage by themselves.

One of the most pressing and urgent concerns I encounter with parents in my practice as a systemic family psychotherapist is the fact that they do not know how to prevent their teenage son/daughter from spending so much time on their smartphones or games. A recent report portrayed that teenagers are spending on average nine hours on their devices a day. This is an alarming statistic that should serve as a wake-up call to every parent, teacher, clinician and policy-maker working with teenagers. We need to look at how technology is impacting the world of our children. Parents must talk to their children about the time they spend on these devices and they must promote a healthy policy that protects them. These devices are only going to become more sophisticated, but we must decide the nature of our children's relationship with them.

The Impact of Nighttime Use of Digital Devices

Blue light from our devices impacts on melatonin production. This is the hormone that promotes sleep. We all have an internal clock, known as the circadian clock, which regulates the amount of sleep we get, and when we view our screens late at night this internal clock is interrupted.

I have observed over the years how more and more teenagers are presenting with exhaustion, low mood and poor motivation in our classrooms. In my research and conversations with teenagers around this modern phenomenon they have outlined to me how they habitually check their phones during the night, which impacts on their energy and enthusiasm for the day ahead. One student explained, 'I know it's probably nothing but if my phone flashes during the night I cannot resist checking it; I have to see what it is and then when it turns out to be nothing I wonder why I checked it at all.' When we examine what this student is describing a very worrying picture develops. Scientists believe that receiving messages on our technological devices stimulates dopamine, which functions as a neurotransmitter in the brain, essentially making us feel good or arousing us so that we want to feel more. Therefore, we get caught in the cycle of sending out and receiving meaningless messages because they are satisfying for a moment. However, when we get stuck in a pattern of compulsion which impacts on our mood we are moving rapidly and dangerously on a trajectory towards addiction. Parents are becoming increasingly aware of this development but are at a loss as how to deal with it.

Practical Tips for Parents
Turn Off Notifications

- Dopamine fires more when there is an unpredictability of outcome. For example, a late-night message that is unsolicited is far too much excitement for the brain to ignore. As parents you must check the settings on your child's phone and set them so any message that is received does not ping after a certain time.
- Eliminate as many visual and auditory cues as possible.
- Make sure your child does not have access to a phone after a certain time. Get them an alarm clock so that they are not using their phone as their only wake-up call, therefore allowing for the removal of the phone from the room at night.
- You must remove all technology from the bedroom. This should be a non-negotiable boundary. But you must do it too. We have to model the behaviour we want our children to exhibit.
- Be consistent with your policy. Teenagers have a heightened sense of fairness and justice. You cannot tell your child not to use their phone when you are modelling the same behaviour.

Self-Deception

One of the most frequent recurring ideas I hear in my work with teenagers around mobile phone usage in the home is this idea of self-deception: 'My Dad tells me that I'm spending too much time on my phone, but he spends way more time than me'. We have to be careful of the behaviour we are modelling for our children. It is a common scene in any restaurant in the country – a family out for a meal, the children are quietly watching their tablets, while the parents are scrolling through their smartphones. When parents come to me and ask 'how can I stop my child from spending so much time on their phone?' I ask them a very simple series of questions:

- What is the pattern in the family for using phones?
- What is your policy like? And do you stick to it?
- What would your children be doing if they were not on their devices?

These questions can often be very difficult for parents to answer because they illuminate the power the family system has in maintaining the homeostasis of the problem.

Our children are not receiving the 8–10 hours of sleep recommended for their bodies and minds to be healthy and rested for the day ahead. This fact is obvious to anyone working in the modern school system. We must, as parents, develop a sensible policy that allows for teenagers to use technology while also educating them on the importance of technology-free time so that their bodies and minds can get some well-needed rest.

* * *

In my work with teenagers, I coordinate a charity project to the Philippines. Every summer I head off with around 24 teenage boys from Catholic University School to work with the children of the Philippines. It really is a wonderful experience for everyone involved. The premise behind the trip is to create a cultural and educational exchange that is mutually beneficial for our boys and the beautiful children of Davao. Because we are working in a deprived area there isn't the opportunity for the boys to be on their devices all the time; in fact they have very little screen time during the two-and-a-half weeks they are there. They are only allowed on their phone for twenty minutes a night to message home to tell their families how things are going. They are not permitted Snapchat, Instagram or any other superficial social media outlets. The reason I don't want them on their devices is to show them what it is like to live free from them. In my experience, they have really never had to live without their devices so they don't know what it is like to just plug out and be in the world. And I observe them in the Philippines living like teenagers of previous generations. They are more interested, more connected to each other and, in my observation, more content. Before we leave to make the long journey home to Ireland, I ask the boys how they found living without technology and I am always struck by what they tell me. In nearly all cases the students excitedly describe how, after the initial shock, they didn't really miss technology at all and how freeing it was to not think about their device all the time. We have to help our children break the relentless checking of their devices and model for them a healthy relationship with technology. Devices are here to stay, there is no doubt about that fact, but we must control the amount of contact time they have with their devices because if we don't they will spend an inordinate amount of time on them, which is not good for their physical or mental health.

Case Study

The Higgins family were referred to me by their GP because the family was experiencing problems with their teenage daughter, Michelle. She was fifteen years old and her parents were quite adamant that there was very little they could do to open up communication with their daughter. The first meeting was particularly problem-saturated.

Mother: Well, the reason we are here is because we can't keep going the way we are going as a family.
Father: Things are not good, it's almost like we can't stand to be around each other.
Mother: It's so unpleasant; the atmosphere in the house is awful.
(Michelle is doing her best to look disengaged from the session. And she rolls her eyes every so often.)
Richard: Can you describe what happens in the house that makes the atmosphere so awful?
Mother: She just won't talk to us. We never know what mood she is going to be in. It's like we are constantly walking on

eggshells. And I seem to always say the wrong thing. We're at the end of our tether with her.
Father: I'm not sure what is normal teenage stuff and what is not normal. It doesn't feel normal, that's for sure.
Richard: Michelle, do you agree with your parents' description of how things are in the house?
Michelle: Yeah, I guess so.
Richard: What do you think makes the atmosphere so awful?
Michelle: I don't know.
Richard: What would you like the atmosphere to be like?
Michelle: I don't know. Different.
(Her parents are smiling at her reticence.)
Richard: Can you describe what it is like for you in the house?
Michelle: I think my parents overreact a lot.
Richard: In what way?
Michelle: I'm in Third Year now so I have a lot of work to do. I don't get home until after six because they have me signed up for after-school study and when I get home I'm tired. That's all, I don't want to talk.
Mother: I don't think it's too much to ask my daughter how her day was.
Michelle: But whatever I say is never enough for you; just yesterday I told you about that thing that happened and you followed me around the whole night asking me about it.
Mother: I was worried about you.
(Michelle heaves a deep sigh.)
Richard: When are things better in the house?
Mother: At the weekend the tension doesn't seem to be there that much.
Richard: Would you agree Michelle?
Michelle: Yeah, but that's because I don't have to get up so early.
Richard: Do you think the early mornings impact on your mood?
Michelle: Yeah, of course. During the week I have to get up at 6 a.m. if I want to be on time for school. And I don't leave school until 6 p.m. I'm wrecked.

Richard: What time do you go to bed at?
(There is a palpable silence in the room. Michelle looks at her mother and smiles. They both laugh.)
Richard: What's making you smile at each other?
Father: They both go to bed very late.
Mother: Well, I'm a bad sleeper so I like to read before I go to sleep.
Michelle: Yeah Mum; you stay up way later than me.
Richard: What time would be normal for you to go to sleep, Michelle?
Michelle: I don't know, about 11 p.m.?
Father: In fairness Michelle, it's a lot later than that. Last night you were pottering around the house at 2 a.m. I heard you.
Michelle: How could you hear me if you were asleep?
Father: I was awake. (He looks at his wife.)
Michelle: I forgot I had PE so I had to get up and get my gear ready.
Richard: How did you remember you had PE?
Mother: Her friend messaged her.
Richard: What time would this have been?
Michelle: 12 a.m.
Mother: They message each other nearly all night; I hear her phone pinging away.
Michelle: You're up too.
Richard: So what time would you eventually go to sleep?
Michelle: Around … (she pauses)
Father: Be honest.
Michelle: 1 or 2.
Richard: And what time do you get up for school, did you say?
Michelle: 6 a.m.
Richard: So you're getting around four hours' sleep during the weeknights?
Father: If that, I'd say.
Mother: Ah, she is!
Richard: What's your policy in the house in relation to technological devices?

(Michelle laughs.)
Mother: I tell her to turn off her phone before going to bed.
Richard: Does that work?
Mother: No.
Michelle: You're worse than me. She wakes up in the middle of the night to go on her iPad.
Mother: I can't sleep sometimes.
Richard: What would it mean as a family to have a policy whereby there is a rule in the house that after a certain time, no one is allowed on devices?
Michelle: She'd find it harder than me.
Mother: No I wouldn't.
(The father smiles.)
Mother: Does that mean I can read again at night?
Richard: Whom are you asking that question to?
Mother: He doesn't let me read because the light wakes him up.
Father: Well, I need to sleep.
Mother: The iPad doesn't wake him up.
Richard: Who would be most put out by the rule?
Michelle: Mum, by far.
(They all laugh.)

Case Study Explained

In this case study we can clearly see the kind of pattern that the family are caught in. The mother and father believe that their daughter's behaviour is symptomatic of some wider issue and that it is making family life unbearable. Therefore, the problem is clearly located within the daughter. She causes the issues in the house and she is the reason there is tension. However, as the conversation unfolds it becomes very clear that both mother and daughter are not getting the sufficient amount of sleep required to function properly during the weekdays. Their lack of sleep is leading to irritability and conflict in the house. The fact that there is no policy around technological device usage in the house allows for both mother and daughter to access their phones excessively. Michelle is only getting around four hours of sleep. This is a very common dilemma in many houses in Ireland today. Children are coming into school fatigued more than ever and this is causing serious problems with behaviour and academic performance. Michelle's mother was slow to introduce a technology policy because she knew that she would also have to give up using her iPad at night. As I said earlier, teenagers have a heightened sense of injustice. The family policy around devices must stand for everyone in the house if it is to be successful. Parents must ask themselves, what am I doing to contribute to the issue that is occurring in the house? If you don't have a policy in your house, ask yourself this difficult question – why not? The answer maybe a little more complex than you would like to think.

Things for Parents to Remember

Remember children crave boundaries. They need them to feel safe. The teenage years are a time when they test those boundaries to see how flexible they actually are. It is important that you show your child that the boundaries are there to protect them and that they are non-negotiable. Research highlights very clearly that when a teenager feels they are not safe or not protected by boundaries the potential for harm through risky behaviour and poor judgement increases significantly.

Remember, be *by* your child's side, not *on* it. I will repeat this phrase many times over the course of this book. Parents often make the mistake of trying to be their child's best friend. They often over-identify with them and become outraged when their child is not picked for the basketball team or doesn't get the leading role in the school play. But parents should ask themselves why are they having such a strong reaction to this. I think you will find that this perceived rejection of your child is bringing up stuff from your own childhood. This may be an uncomfortable reality to confront. But, what our children really need is to feel that we are there to protect them and to support them on this wonderful journey. They need to feel that we will really listen to them when they tell us something about their world. And we won't judge or overreact but rather encourage. When we judge and become irate about some issue they are experiencing we only heighten their sense of anxiety. Because we are implicitly telling them that they are right to be worried about that issue. I will talk about anxiety in Chapter 8 and how you can support your child during a difficult time.

Task

If you are having conflict in your house about the amount of time spent on mobile phones or technological devices try the following task.

- Set a boundary. You must allow for the peaceful co-existence of technology and family time. Clearly write out the rules, which everyone must follow. Stick them somewhere all the family can see, like the fridge.
- Ensure that there is time set aside for your teenager to access their social media.
- Do something spontaneous with your child that doesn't require technology. A modern teenager's world can be quite regimented between school and home. Spontaneity will always be welcomed by teenagers. Maybe decide as a family that you are all going to leave your devices at home before you go out.
- Rotate who decides what you are going to do as a family during this family time.
- Make a journal of what worked and what didn't work.

Just a Thought

When you think about your child, what comes into your mind? Privileged? Into technology? They don't know how good they have it? If only they knew what it was like for me? Soft? Snowflake? The list could go on and on. I grew up in a time when teenagers were either known as 'grunge heads' or 'techno heads', but I remember thinking at the time how it didn't really catch all of us because I was neither of those descriptors, so what was I? A Cure head? Maybe. I liked The Beatles so maybe I was a mop top, but I didn't have the hair-cut. I definitely wasn't a Mod or a Rocker and glam rock didn't do it for me, or at least I couldn't find shoulder pads growing up in Cork, so again, what was I? Oh yeah, I was a teenager growing up in the 90s. And that was kind of 'rad'. Each generation has its own slang and each generation gets looked on with confusion and suspicion by the passing one. But these teenagers are really getting a hard time of it because they are more vocal about what it is they are feeling and going through. When Lear is out at the cliffs with Gloucester he asks him how he sees the world now that he is blind. Gloucester replies, 'I see it feelingly.' So our teenagers are experiencing the world in a more feeling way. Surely this must be seen as progress? After all, they wouldn't be able to express the depths of their emotions if their parents (who were once 'grunge heads' or 'techno heads') hadn't instilled in them that they were safe to express those very feelings and thoughts. Or if they hadn't received the message that maybe life isn't as simple as our binary system once told us it was. So why have we turned on them? Maybe it's jealousy: why do they get to be the ones to live life how they want to? The answer is because we, the parents, told them to expect more and to question accepted norms.

***

In my work I talk to adolescents every day, both in a clinical setting and in the school system. And I often ask them how they feel about the way they are viewed by the adult world. What I hear is very interesting. They generally become animated about it and express deep annoyance at the hypocrisy that underpins the label 'snowflakes' – because they see that label for what it is: a way to diminish them and to rubbish their feelings as precious and irrelevant. Life for the modern teenager is different than for any other generation that has gone before. The proliferation of technology and ubiquitous internet means that new vistas of communication have become possible. Language may be more abbreviated and functional and how they go about socialising has changed, but other than that the teenager of today has the same needs as every other teenager that has gone before. Yet, the media is interested in painting these children as some sort of alien race that parents find almost impossible to relate to. Every coming generation is treated with intolerance by adults who do not have the skills or interest to listen to them and to understand what it is they are going through.

And when we don't understand something we often reject it as being useless or having no value.

This book is designed to show you how to think about the teenager in your home in a different way. Things are different for them, but they still have the same needs all other generations of teenagers had. They need love and support like all of us did, and now they also need us to understand the impact technology is having on their social and familial worlds. And we have to rise to that challenge. Try not to think of your child in terms of labels, because they will not respond well to it and they will see you as just another adult who views them incorrectly.

These 'snowflakes' didn't arrive by some polar vortex; we created them by how we parented them. We should be proud that they have the confidence to express how they experience the world. And even prouder that they see the world like Gloucester did, in a feeling way.

THOUGHTS ON CHANGING BEHAVIOUR

There is this idea in Jungian psychology known as circumambulation, and it refers to the notion of how we move towards reaching full potential. I find myself talking about this theory a lot in my practice with parents of teenage children because parents often seek out therapy after the teenager in the house has done something troubling or failed to succeed in an endeavour. The reason I mention circumambulation is because Jung believed that development doesn't occur in a straight line. In fact, he stated that 'there is no linear evolution, there is only a circumambulation of the self.' This means that development and reaching potential isn't going to be a perfect adventure and those failures are there to teach us something on the way to meaningful growth. So, we have to rethink how our children develop and evolve, because it doesn't happen in a perfect way. There will be many mistakes along the road. When we realise this it can help us manage our reactions to our children's failings, which will place us in a more supportive role. None of us want to be that critical voice in our child's mind that is destructive and stops them from reaching their full potential. Think about how your child learned to walk – was it perfect? Or did they take many messy and clumsy steps as their brains tried to calibrate and figure out how to balance upright? Think about that toddler as your child moves through adolescence. They will not get everything right; they will make clumsy and awkward moves because they are calibrating all the time.

If we think about the archetypal hero's journey it illuminates Jung's concept clearly. The hero doesn't get there without difficulty, they don't become the saviour without losing or failing along the way. It is in these failures that the hero becomes something truly great because they have gained the important insight that falling short is part of becoming great. We must all come to that understanding about our children and our aspirations for them to improve. Many of the teenagers I meet put themselves under incredible pressure to be perfect and to meet every goal they set for themselves. They come into the session visibly deflated, shoulders shrugged and head down; they look beaten. They come armed, though, with a very important question: how do I change my behaviour? That is such a good question. Let's just say they are lazy and want to be more productive or they want to know how to study more and go out less. I talk to them about the effective six stages of change.

In the 1980s two professors from Rode Island University devised a six-stage theoretical model for changing and modifying behaviour. Remember, all behaviour can be changed. There is no doubt about it: habits form easily and can be very tricky to break but they can be broken with the right approach. The stages are as follows:

1. *Pre-contemplation:* This is the unconscious moments before we realise we need to change. We are active in the behaviour, such as excessive gaming on our devices more than we would like.
2. *Contemplation:* We begin to realise we need to change. So, let's just say you're not happy with the number of hours your child is spending on the game. You must calmly point this out to your child. The chances are they will have noticed it themselves and are already in the contemplation stage. They just might not admit to it.
3. *Preparation:* This is a very important stage. I had a client recently come to me about his smoking habit. His eight-year-old

daughter had come to him and asked him to stop smoking because she was worried about his health. He knew he needed to stop but had failed so many times before he was terrified he would let her down. We talked about circumambulation and the notion of these failed attempts teaching him something, and we planned that he would have to replace smoking with something else more positive and healthy. He joined his local tennis club. There was a lot of preparation before he began to stop smoking. I think this is where many of us fall down. We fail to prepare adequately. So, let's say your son is spending too much time on gaming. Before you bring in the notion of stopping the behaviour you must plan to introduce an alternative activity. A question I ask parents before we move into this stage of behaviour change is, if your child wasn't gaming what would they be doing? If you cannot think of an answer to that question you are not ready to help your child change their behaviour.
4. *Action:* This is when the habit is stopped.
5. *Maintenance:* In the example above, going to the tennis club was how my client maintained his life free from smoking. Parents often introduce a family activity that the child chooses. This way they are doing something else instead of gaming. If you just remove the games without planning an alternative you will bring a considerable amount of conflict into the house.
6. *Relapse:* When I tell clients that there may be moments of relapse and not to be fearful of that because they are a natural part of development they become relieved. I bring in Jungian psychology again here and describe the hero's journey; it's not a straight line. Generally clients who relapse either go back to the first stage and stay there or move directly into stages four and five again. So, if your child begins to over-game again don't become overly concerned. You simply need to analyse what went wrong in the stages that didn't allow for your child to alter their behaviour. Maybe you didn't allow for the existence of both gaming and family time. It's about getting the balance right. It's not about getting rid of the games. Your child will,

more than likely, outgrow the game. But you have to help them to manage their relationship with it as they move to adulthood.

We are only prisoners to our patterns of behaviour as long as we do not see them. Once we realise our children need help with a particular habit we must set a plan in place that will allow for a successful outcome.

3

Building Levels of Communication with a Screenager

'To win back my youth, there is nothing I wouldn't do – except take exercise, get up early, or be a useful member of the community.' (Oscar Wilde)

While at first glance this may seem like a flippant comment, I think Wilde is touching on something we all experience as parents of teenagers. They can be quite reticent, perhaps even lethargic, and in some cases reluctant to take part in the family. This can be an exasperating time for parents.

During childhood children generally look up to their parents as a colossus of strength and knowledge. This can be a very rewarding time for both parents and children as the relationship develops along mutually beneficial and clearly defined lines; the child needs the parent and the parent has a very clear role to fulfil. However, as children move into their teenage years they tend to rely more on their peer group than their parents. This shift in relational dynamics can cause stress in the house as parents struggle to come to terms with this new relationship. In fact, in my experience, parents often come to view adolescence as a time of loss. They can feel hurt, as their once wide-eyed, chatty child no longer seeks them out as a source of advice and companionship. These hurt feelings can often move into anger as their child's secrecy or rebellious behaviour challenges their competencies. Parents can feel uncomfortable with how they have been positioned in the house; they often describe feeling like an interloper in their child's life. I find reframing the idea of loss for parents an important part of the work I do. I tell them that adolescence is not really about loss but about being together differently. And more importantly, it is only temporary and the relationship will change again as their teenager moves into adulthood.

Parents often ask me what can they do to improve communication with their teenage son or daughter. And I generally commence by explaining that adolescence is a time of exploration. It's a time when children develop their own concept of self, when they move towards independence and away from the shadow of their parents. During adolescence teenagers test the boundaries and challenge authority. However, it is important that during these challenges parents hold their child. The type of holding I'm describing here is empathetic, not rigid but also not without consequences. A child must know that there are boundaries and that when they challenge them they move slightly to allow for the challenge/resistance but that ultimately these boundaries (while not being absolutely rigid) will not give in. This type of holding allows for the adolescent to explore safely while also understanding that there are clear boundaries around certain areas that will not be compromised.

Reframing the Sense of Loss

Adolescence can be a time of loss for both parents and child: 'I just don't know who John is anymore' or 'when will that lovely boy come back to us?' or 'he was such a great child, where has he gone?'

I get asked these types of questions a lot by very anxious parents. And the sadness in the room for the loss of their once beautiful, garrulous child is tangible. Equally, when talking with adolescents about this theme they often feel the same way. They feel the loss that their parents feel but also their own guilt around that loss and their own sense of loss around the hero figure that is no more. For the first nine or so years a child generally looks up to their mother and father as an infallible colossus. In adolescence they rely more heavily on their peer group. If a parent has difficulty adapting to a changing family environment during a child's adolescence, the adolescent may perceive less parental support or love and be more prone to developing depression or other mental health difficulties. Similarly, as an adolescent struggles to manage the emotional, physical and social changes that accompany the transition to adolescence they might experience depressive symptoms (e.g. sullenness, irritability, diminished energy) that frustrate or dishearten a parent and negatively affect that parent's ability to communicate with their child. Managing both parents' and child's expectations of each other is an important feature of working with a family attempting to build levels of communication. Parents often come to view adolescence as a 'moving away' from them; I like to reframe it and instead talk about it in terms of 'being together differently' or describing it as a time of 'discovery' for the family. This kind of reframing conversation can help both parent and child to see their position differently. And help them to overcome feelings of loss that the family system may be experiencing, which can actually improve communication between all members in that family system.

The Wider World of the Adolescent

I often think about Prince Hamlet and his situation as a very interesting case study for adolescent mental health. Hamlet's father dies and his mother marries his uncle very quickly. This causes Hamlet to dramatically change his view of the world and women in general. Of course, finding out that the man who is now sleeping with his mother actually murdered his father and usurped the throne causes Hamlet an emotional and physical paralysis. So Hamlet finds it nearly impossible to express the inner turmoil of his emotional storm. I often talk with young teenagers who find it almost impossible to express what it is they are going through. And I often find my mind drifting to the story of *Hamlet* and how he communicates aspects of his story that trouble him the most.

When Hamlet calls on the players to render a speech from 'Aeneas' tale to Dido', his choice of subject offers some obvious parallels to his own situation. Hecuba, the archetypal grieving queen, is an effective contrast to Gertrude. Pyrrhus' vengeance for his father's death is a reminder of the duty laid on Hamlet, as well as on Laertes and Fortinbras. This request by Hamlet speaks directly to the utter inner turmoil of his mind, and elucidates for the audience many of the complicated themes that have not been directly spoken about in the text. Often adolescents find it easier to talk about music, film or literature than the issues they are experiencing. In the words of the dull, ill-fated Polonius, 'by indirections' we can 'find directions out'.

This use of 'indirection' is an important approach when working with adolescents. Over the years I have had many conversations about people such as Kurt Cobain, Jim Morrison, John Lennon, Marilyn Manson, Eminem, NWA, Sylvia Plath, Amy Winehouse, Alex Turner or whatever group or person is current at that particular moment. It is important to get a sense of the adolescents' world. What are they feeding on? What messages are they interested in hearing? Whom are they receiving them from? And why? Conversations around music and literature have proven to be very fruitful to me in my work with adolescents. And they certainly help to build levels of communication in the therapeutic setting. They often help me to gauge the inner working of the adolescent's mind, as they often reveal something that the conversation might not. Or what I have also found is that the adolescent might be reticent or embarrassed to give words to a certain feeling or emotion. However a certain song or poem might say it for them, therefore allowing for the conversation to take place in an indirect way. So when you are trying to open up the lines of communication with your child, think about what the music they are listening to or the books they are reading are telling you. What is grabbing their interest at that particular time? I'm not suggesting that you have to get into gangster rap, if that is what your child is listening to, but maybe you could ask yourself the question, why are they listening to that type of content? And what are those lyrics saying that my child is interested in? It is important to stay in touch with your chid as they move through the tumultuous years of adolescence. All the research is there to show us that children who feel like they are not being minded or held are statistically far more likely to engage in anti-social behaviour.

Tips for Building Communication with Your Screenager

- Identify the times they are more likely to open up. If your teenager is not particularly chatty in the morning (don't panic, it's common!), perhaps don't push the conversation at that time. Wait for a moment you think they are more likely to chat – maybe at dinner or after sports practice.
- Make it clear to your child that you are always available for a chat. Just say something as simple as 'you know if you ever want to chat about anything, I'm here for you.' Often the teenagers I meet explain how they didn't go to their parents with a problem because they thought they wouldn't listen or that they were too busy. So it's important to let them know that you will listen.
- If they do come to you with something, make sure you do not overreact to the piece of information they give you. For example, I had a child recently tell me that they couldn't go to their parents about the issue of cyber-bullying because they were worried that their parents would ban them from their phone altogether. When parents overreact the only message they are giving their child is that they are not a safe person to go to with an issue.

- Stay involved in their life. Keep up with whom they are friendly with and talk to them about their friends. And invite their friends to your house and chat with them. The more involved you are the more you will have to talk to them about.
- And try to remember what it was like to be a teenager. Not all of us have experienced depression or cyber-bullying, but we have all been teenagers and we all know what it was like for us. So try to recall that, and ask yourself, what would I have responded well to and what didn't I respond well to?

Adolescence is undoubtedly a challenging time for both teenager and parent. We must not allow ourselves to be placed on the periphery of our children's life. We must stay involved and provide them with a shelter for the stormy years ahead. While we should never tell our teenagers 'it's only a phase', the reality is it generally does pass and things eventually will return to a peaceful rhythm in the house. Try not to look at adolescence as a time of loss but, rather, think of it as a time of exploration and a time where your child is forging their own identity on their journey through life. And they're taking you along for the ride.

4

Approaches to Gaming

The World Health Organisation (WHO) in June 2018 recognised a new kind of mental health condition. For many parents and psychotherapists alike it is an all-too-familiar aliment, one that has been present in the family and clinic for many years now. It is a disorder that psychotherapists have had difficulty finding language for, because up until 2018 it had not been classified. But we all knew it was there. Because we have seen the devastation a family experiences when a member is suffering with the illness. In my experience, its presence has destroyed relationships, family holidays, school attendance, personal hygiene, health and social interactions, to mention but a few of the consequences of this particular aliment. The name of this new condition: gaming disorder. It is characterised by 'a pattern of persistent or recurrent gaming behaviour'. It shares many of the same commonalties as other addictive compulsions such as gambling or alcoholism. A recent study found that when individuals are engaged in internet gaming, due to the immersive quality of the games, 'certain pathways in their brains are triggered in the same direct and intense way that a drug addict's brain is affected by a particular substance'. The American Psychiatric Association went further and stated that 'gaming prompts a neurological response that influences feelings of pleasure and reward, and the result, in the extreme, is manifested as addictive behaviour'. That is to say, not all teenagers playing games are addicts but what the APA has outlined should serve as a loud warning bell to all parents of teenagers who are currently concerned about their child's gaming habits.

In my clinical experience, parents often come looking for help when the behaviour has reached an intolerable level. They delineate how they have been concerned for many years but never knew what to do. And now the behaviour has reached a level where it is not only causing their child serious problems such as school refusal, it is also eroding the family structure itself, so they need professional help. This has many similarities to any family living with a drug addict. I am often faced with desperate parents looking for solutions to help their family from complete collapse. Unfortunately, it is very difficult to break a habit when it has become so entrenched; of course it's not impossible but it is difficult, so spotting the early warning signs that your child is moving on a trajectory towards addiction is vital if there is to be a successful outcome. And parenting your child's gaming habits is just another facet of modern-day parenting.

SIGNS THAT GAMING ADDICTION IS FORMING

- Spending increasing time in their bedroom, and not meeting friends in real life. If you notice that your child is making excuses for not meeting up with their friends or is spending an inordinate amount of time in the bedroom, it could be an early warning sign that they are becoming addicted to online gaming.
- A decrease in appetite. I had one client tell me that he had forgotten to eat for over 24 hours because he was so consumed

with the game. And this is not an isolated incident. Many students I talk to about online gaming outline how they could easily go 16 hours without eating. They become so engrossed in the game that they forget about basic human functions. Something as simple as personal hygiene can become an issue when addiction is present. This should tell you how immersive these games are and how our children need to be minded as they navigate this world. Games are here to stay and they are going to become more immersive as these designers become more sophisticated in their approach to getting your child hooked on the game. So you must be vigilant here.

- They become angry or aggressive when you suggest they leave the bedroom. This is a very clear sign that a dangerous habit is forming. If you notice this, you should seek professional advice. The longer you leave the habit to form the more difficult it is to break. The good news is that all habits can be broken, but the longer they are allowed to exist the more entrenched they become.
- A loss in real-life activities. Often when addiction is forming activities that once brought joy become arduous and joyless. This is a key sign that addiction is present. One of the most striking feature about this new type of gaming is the isolation over-playing brings into a young adult's life. I see the total fallout in my work. And this is not just a child's issue. I see adults from 25 to 50 struggling with this issue. And it can bring about the total collapse of a once healthy and functioning person.

The very nature of many of these online games is designed to be addictive. When we think about gambling, the addictive compulsion is about risk and reward. The potential to win money negates the reality of what losing the money will mean for the gambler. So they lose control of reality. Many online games are designed around the same premise: you can win the highest points or defeat the game, or you can be the last man standing. The creative forces involved in this world understand only too well what all this means for the young mind navigating this murky landscape. For in a teenager's bid to beat the game the designers have devised an insidious way to make money: they sell additional content to help the gamer beat the game. This drive to gain the highest points or defeat the game can, for some teenagers, become an all-consuming activity to the detriment of their mental and physical health. And parents need to be able to spot the warnings signs because, for some of these game designers, they are shooting fish in a barrel when it comes to getting your child hooked on their product.

IDENTITY AND THE GAME

For many parents this is all too familiar. They've probably known for some time that their child's relationship with the game is unhealthy. They've watched their child display all the signs I have just mentioned in silent disbelief, or perhaps not even silent and there has been much conflict in the house. It can be a very unsettling and challenging time watching your child become addicted to something you don't understand. And because you didn't understand it, you probably didn't know what to do about what was unfolding in front of your own eyes. Maybe you sought professional advice or at the very least maybe you Googled the issue and found that there really isn't much information out there for parents who have a child stuck in a serious compulsive gaming habit. I get invited by schools all over the country to talk to parents about how they can support their child who is over-gaming. Last year, after I had delivered one of those talks, a parent stood up and outlined how all of her three boys were addicted to gaming. She described the total isolation that gaming had brought into their family life. She said she blamed her husband who brought the games into the lives of once very active and happy children. She described the battle to get them to even go and see their grandparents. One of the boys was refusing to go to school. I could tell she was at her wits' end with it all. She also described the pressure it was placing on her relationship with her husband. I could see all the nodding heads of the parents sitting there who recognised the similarities between her story and their own lived experience. Before she sat down she left me with a sentence that has stayed with me since: 'I just want my family back'.

Approaches to Gaming 47

This was such a poignant and profound statement to make and her sadness stayed with me for some time. Many families are struggling with this issue and it can really devastate all that is good and healthy about a particular family unit.

But the good news is that you can get your family back. I have stayed in touch with that lady, and she has put in place many new boundaries around gaming that have had a powerful positive impact on her family life. But it took time; as I said in Chapter 1, when your child has operated free from boundaries you must put them in place one at a time. Too much difference is not good for a child. And that is what this lady did. Her children are back playing sports and the tension in the house has decreased significantly.

Another aspect I have noticed is that a child's reputation is getting caught up in the games. Traditionally speaking, it was the guy or girl who was good at sport whom the other children admired. This was healthy because they went out to training with their friends and exercised and socialised; they were a part of a team, they won and lost together. There was great learning in it and camaraderie. But now the child who is really proficient at the game is receiving that same adulation from their classmates and it is further increasing their desire to play the games compulsively. Because the more they play the more praise they receive. And this is what parents do not understand. Your child wants to play so much because when they go into school they hear all about the kills they had the night before or how they saved their team from annihilation. So, their reputation is caught up in the game. This further compounds the situation and should illuminate why your child needs to be minded when it comes to these games.

PATTERNS OF ADDICTIVE BEHAVIOUR

The first important aspect about all of this that parents should know is that many of these games are designed to be addictive. The very principles of some games are designed in such a way that they hook your child on the product; this is how they make money. Your child is being targeted, in a rather sinister way, by these game designers. But the good news is that you, as the parent, have all the power in this interaction. Just like we wouldn't dream of letting some stranger give our child a dangerous substance, we must apply the same thinking with regards to online games and regulate the amount of time our children engage with them.

When parents first come to me seeking advice about their child who is spending too much time with online gaming, I first of all look at the pattern of behaviour in the family as a whole. I am a systemically trained psychotherapist, which means I always look at the system and how it contributed to the current issue it is labouring with. And one aspect that I find recurring with such an issue is that parents often use games as a parenting tool. We must face our own self-deception as parents before we can truly help our children. Often parents describe, in our early conversations, how happy they were initially because their child was up in their bedroom, free from danger, or so they thought. But while they were spending an inordinate amount of time in the bedroom they were becoming addicted to playing games online. And the parents have come to realise that there is something very wrong with their child's relationship with gaming. So when they ask me what they should do to help their child overcome this dependency on online games, I offer the following advice:

1. Remove games, computers, consoles and phones from your child's bedroom. When the computer is in the bedroom it is almost impossible to monitor successfully the amount of time your child is spending online. I have conversations with teenagers around this issue a lot, and you would be horrified at the amount of time they secretly play their games and the myriad ways they have to get online. But when parents remove the games from the bedroom and place them in a more public area, like the sitting room, they remove the potential for secrecy and allow monitoring to take place. Your child will fight this, but you must be resolute on this issue or else there is no point.
2. You must be consistent with your parenting of this habit. Your child should not be allowed play games for as long as they want. You must set the rules around this and stick to them. If the

rule is after they finish their homework they can play their game for one hour a day, you must stick to it. Children crave boundaries. And when they are firmly established and non-negotiable, your child will understand and follow them. However, it is crucial that both parents are saying the same thing. If one gives in, all that hard work will be in vain. Nothing promotes negative behaviour in children more than inconsistent parenting.

3. Get familiar with the game your child is playing. At the moment the big game they are all playing is *Fortnite*. Any parent with a child between eight and eighteen years of age will be fully aware of this game. It has taken the world by storm with over 125 million players worldwide, with total game revenue for 2018 estimated at $2.4 billion. There is huge money to be made and our children need to be minded while navigating these games. Children can access this game from any device. So understand how they are playing it – Xbox, PlayStation, etc. – and then use the parental controls to limit the length of gaming sessions. A game usually lasts 20 minutes, so you can tell your child they can play three games a day. That way you are not cutting them off mid-game, which will cost them points and reputational damage because they left the game before it was finished. Preventing this from happening will be an important factor for peace in the family home and when your child is clear about how many games they can play, it will take a lot of the conflict out of the family.

4. If you notice that your child goes up to play the game when you are busy making dinner or when you want to watch TV, ask yourself who really has the unhealthy relationship with technology? What I mean by this is that we can easily fall into a comfortable relationship with the games ourselves. We have to beware of the self-deception that often accompanies gaming. Parents can be happy that their child is gaming because it keeps them quiet at a particular time but angry because their child won't stop when they ask them to. So, ask yourself that important question: what is my relationship with the game like and has this helped to maintain the problem?

Parenting your child's online gaming habits is just another feature of modern parenting. When we were young parents were warned about the dangers of using TV as a parenting tool. However, gaming has a far more sinister side to it because there is money to be made. So, as parents you must decide what is a healthy amount of time for your child to spend playing these games. By setting a few concrete boundaries and removing the games from the bedroom, you can find that there can be a harmonious balance for gaming in your teenager's life.

Case Study

The Mahon family came to me because their son's gaming habit had recently caused a huge fight in the family. Paul had refused to attend his cousin's First Holy Communion and his parents were concerned that he was addicted to his games because he wasn't leaving his room. In the initial conversations they described many of the criteria I outlined earlier to recognise the presence of addiction. Paul had stopped eating, his hygiene was poor and he didn't want to leave his room. He had also stopped meeting his friends. This case study is taken from my first conversation with Paul.

Richard: Can you describe an average evening in the house, when you first get home from school?
Paul: Just come in, get something to eat and go to my room.
Richard: Where are Mum and Dad?
Paul: Work probably. Mum might be there, depending on the day; Dad is home latest.
Richard: When Mum is there what is she doing?
Paul: Making dinner, maybe watching TV.
Richard: If you don't go to your room what are you doing?
Paul: Don't know, hang around.
Richard: So most evenings you go to your room?
Paul: Yeah.
Richard: What do you do there?
Paul: Play a few games, homework.
Richard: In what order?

Paul: Play games, then homework, and game again.
Richard: What game do you like?
Paul: *Fortnite*.
Richard: What do you like about it?
Paul: It's fun; it's not serious like other games and my friends all play it.
Richard: Do you buy Vbucks?
Paul: Nah, Mum doesn't give me money for them. I don't need them anyway.
Richard: Have you any other hobbies?
Paul: I like drawing. (Paul takes out a refill pad and shows it to me; it's full of anime drawings.)
Richard: Wow, you're a talented drawer. They're very good. How long have you being doing them?
Paul: Not long.
Richard: So when you're not playing, you're drawing?
Paul: Yeah, I make up my own games.
Richard: How did you get interested in that?
Paul: Don't know, from the games.
Richard: If you weren't playing the games and drawing what would you do with your spare time?
Paul: Don't know, I used to like football but it's boring.
Richard: Did you support anyone?
Paul: Man United.
Richard: They're tough to support at the moment.
Paul: I don't support them anymore.
Richard: What do you do with your family that you enjoy?
Paul: Go for a meal, Eddie Rockets or something.
Richard: What do you like about that?
Paul: The food mainly.
Richard: Do you like being with the family?
Paul: It's okay; Dad's on his phone for most of it, and if my brother acts up he's on my mother's phone. Me and Mum chat a bit.
Richard: Can I ask you how you first got into gaming?
Paul: Got a PlayStation for my ninth birthday.

Richard: What do you like about the games?
Paul: You forget about things.
Richard: What sort of things do you forget about?
Paul: Just things you don't want to think about.
Richard: Can you tell me some of those?
Paul: I don't really want to.
Richard: What would need to happen here for you to tell me, Paul?
Paul: You'd have to promise not to tell my mum.
Richard: Well, I can't promise until I hear it but I can give you my word if it doesn't endanger you or anyone else we can keep it between us.
Paul: I just don't like being at home. It's boring. There is nothing to do and my parents are at me and they love David.
Richard: Thank you for sharing that with me; I know it's not easy to tell someone you have just met something like that, so thank you – you're very brave.
Paul: Thanks.
Richard: What else about home don't you like?
Paul: It's not just home, I don't like school either.
Richard: Okay, can we stay with home for the moment, can you describe a few things you don't like.
Paul: Dad and Mum are always on at me about stuff. They don't like my friends, they think I'm smoking hash and they don't let my friends call over. Dad calls me names too, like 'waste of space' and 'Gameboy'; sometimes I think he is saying 'gayboy' but I think it's 'Gameboy'.
Richard: Okay, I'd imagine that's hard to hear. What do you say when he calls you names?
Paul: Tell him to leave me alone or get out of my room.
Richard: So you stand up for yourself?
Paul: A little, but not too much; Dad gets very angry if I talk back.
Richard: How do you know when Dad is angry?
Paul: He is shouting, name-calling, giving out about everything.
Richard: Like?
Paul: Gaming, homework, hash.

> Richard: Which one upsets you the most?
> Paul: My friends.
> Richard: Does playing the games block this out?
> Paul: Yeah, it does. And I can chat with my friends too.
> Richard: So you meet your friends on the game?
> Paul: Yeah we have a group.
> Richard: If I had a magic wand, what way would things be in the house?
> Paul: My friends could call over and Mum and Dad would stop getting at me all the time. And Dad would chill.
> Richard: Do you play the games all night?
> Paul: Sometimes.
> Richard: How do Mum and Dad get you to stop?
> Paul: They shout about it now and again. That's about it.
> Richard: Are the games in your bedroom?
> Paul: Yeah; don't tell them to take the games out of my room. Anyway Dad watches sport so doesn't want the PlayStation in the siting room.

This piece of conversation is a good microcosm for what is going on in many families around the world. Parents are annoyed with their children for playing the games too much but they are maintaining the issue by how they parent it. Paul's story is similar to many I have heard. Paul is using the game to sooth his emotional distress. There is a lot of tension in this house and gaming is a way to avoid dealing with this stress. Also the social aspect to modern-day gaming is not being recognised by the family. Their parental competencies are being tested and they are meeting that challenge by reverting to name-calling and shouting, neither of which is a desirable way to respond to your child's issues. But when our competencies are tested we often revert to how we were treated as children; it's our default position. Often parents describe a certain interaction they have with their child and say things like 'I never thought I'd turn into that type of parent.' The type of parent they are generally referring to here is their own parents. They have strived so hard to parent their own child differently but they have been programmed with this default setting that when their competencies get pushed it triggers the setting and they are left baffled as to how they could have acted or reacted in such a negative way. So, you have to hear yourself and the way you communicate to your child. When I discussed some of the things that Paul described to the parents they were really horrified to hear his experience. The father broke down and sobbed. He described his own experience living with a very dominating father who called him names when he was angry. His wife said that she had been subjected to many years of name-calling and she didn't like when he called their children names. But she didn't know how to express it to her husband because she was nervous of his reaction. And Paul was avoiding them both by being in his room, but he was also meeting those friends they didn't allow into the house online. Therefore, the parents were creating the perfect situation for Paul to become immersed in his games. We have to examine our own behaviours before we can start to look at our children's. This is not about blame but rather about understanding how the issue was created in the first place and how the family has helped to maintain it. When we know this we can easily develop a parental strategy that will have a successful outcome.

Things to Think About

- Are you using the game to parent your child? Is there a comfortable dynamic in the house? Are they quietly playing the game upstairs while you are having some downtime, watching TV? If so, who really has the unhealthy relationship with the game? You cannot outsource your parenting responsibilities.
- Are you letting them over-play the game because you know it makes them happy, and you do not see them as much as you would like, due to work and financial commitments? Are you parenting from a position of guilt?
- If they weren't playing the game what would they be doing?
- Think of gaming as avoidance: what does the game block out?
- Are the boundaries in the house clear and concise?

Gaming is here to stay, but it is just another challenge that parents must meet with resolve and forethought. It is not about taking away the games entirely but about creating an environment that allows for the existence of both gaming and family time. Your child will game, but you decide the nature of that relationship. And when you have a boundary in place that holds the child, that child will learn how to play their game in a healthy way that is free from compulsion and excess.

5

Online Pornography

The recent proliferation of internet−enabled technology has dramatically changed the way adolescents encounter and consume sexually explicit material. Such material, traditionally only sourced through magazines, videos or at the end of a personal computer which was attached to a telephone line, is now, in today's world, easier than ever to access. The ubiquity of the internet and the multitude of electronic devices available to teenagers, such as laptops, mobile phones and video game consoles, means that sexually explicit material is only ever a few clicks away. In my work in schools I have worked closely with management to address this pressing and urgent concern. The reality is students are accessing extreme hard-core pornography on their devices. While most schools, at this stage, have a mobile phone policy in the school, the fact remains that explicit images and extreme pornographic content are only ever a click away from your children's fingers. Viewing such material can have damaging and long-lasting effects on a young mind. So, the question we are left asking ourselves as parents, teachers and clinicians is, how do we protect our children from viewing these images?

While it is developmentally normal for adolescents to have sexual curiosity, the reality seems to be that these normal sexual curiosities are being satiated by extreme and highly explicit material. In my practice, I have noticed over the years the increasing pressure on young girls and boys to send explicit images to each other. Does this trend speak to the fact that exposure to such explicit material seems to be normalising highly provocative and risky behaviour for our teenagers? I have often wondered, after I have a conversation with a young adult about their use of pornography, whether or not habitual pornography usage irrevocably changes how a young person views sexual relationships? And does it damage how they view intimacy by changing their perception of sex as primarily physical and casual rather than affectionate and relational? As a psychotherapist, teacher and more importantly as a father of three young girls, I personally find this recent development quite worrying. There is a dearth of research on this extremely sensitive topic, but in my work as a systemic psychotherapist I have met many couples who have come to counselling because pornography has significantly impacted on their marital life. When I talk to the member of the couple who is experiencing the difficulty they nearly always delineate how early exposure to pornography disturbed the way they have come to view sexual intimacy. This has led me to conclude that preventing our children from coming into contact with sexually explicit material significantly increases their ability to have normal and healthy relationships in the future. And, as the parents, we must vigilantly watch what they are watching on their phones, because that is where they are accessing these pornographic images.

What Teenagers Say

"I sent it because I didn't want to be called 'dry'."

These were the words of a desperate young girl who came to me for counselling. Her entire social world had collapsed because of her desire to fit in. She had suffered massive psychological trauma after an image she had sent to a boy went around her social circle. This had left a devastating and indelible mark not only on the girl's psyche, but also on the boy who had sent it. As we know, and rightly so, the proliferation of sexually explicit images of minors is a very serious act in today's world. The boy, who was slightly older, could have potentially been faced with a criminal record as a sex offender. This is not an isolated incident and the ramifications for both parties were particularly upsetting and traumatic. So, we have to educate our children about the consequences of sending explicit images over their devices, and also the legal implications for having such images on their devices.

Schools are finally beginning to address this serious issue. However, for this to be truly effective, we need to employ a joint system approach – where the family and the school work together to educate our children about the dangers of pornography and the difference between online sexually explicit images and real-life intimacy. Education is the key to a successful outcome with this sensitive topic. And often we do not like to talk about a topic like this because it might make us uncomfortable, but we need to get over our own awkwardness because it is a conversation that your child needs to have. In my experience, girls are coming under increasing pressure to send compromising pictures of themselves to potential boyfriends. I am seeing this more and more in my practice and the impact on their mental health once they have sent it is devastating. Because once it is sent it is out there forever. Snapchat is particularly insidious as the messages sent on this app disappear after five seconds. So it's very hard to keep an eye on because there is no record of the activity. However, in my conversations with young adults around this topic I often hear them explain how they mistakenly thought the image they sent was deleted because the person they sent it to didn't take a screenshot but what they subsequently discovered was that the person they sent the image to took a picture of the image on someone else's phone and now that image has been disseminated around their social group. The ramifications of this can be totally overwhelming for a young mind, and adolescents can feel like they have no way out of this situation without taking drastic action. And unfortunately there are many families out there left picking up the pieces after something like this has visited their home, so keeping your child educated about this topic is crucial and keeping an eye on their social media accounts, especially image-based ones such as Instagram, and monitoring the kind of images they are uploading is important. Self-esteem is often at the root of a young girl's reason for sending an explicit image to someone.

TIPS FOR PARENTS

- *Set your search engine to restricted mode.* If your child uses services like YouTube be sure you have set the 'safe' mode on those platforms as well, especially if they are under 12 years of age.
- *Switch from using regular YouTube to YouTube Kids, which only contains family-friendly content.* I had a parent tell me recently that her child had viewed violent and sexual images on YouTube and hadn't been able to sleep since. She hadn't realised that YouTube Kids was available. It is important that you research which are the safest platforms for your child to be viewing content on.
- *Use family safety tools and services.* These tools allow parents to set specific filters to block types of content they find inappropriate.
- *Randomly check your child's browser history.* There are a number of phrases that teenagers use which get around pornography filters, like 'Netflix and chill', which is slang for sex. If you encounter strange phrases click on them and see where they bring you.
- *Talk to other parents.* See what steps they are taking to protect their children. I know it is a sensitive issue but the more we talk about it the more we demystify it, which might actually serve to take some of the secrecy and excitement out of it.

The arrival of ubiquitous internet has meant that sexually explicit material is only ever a click away from our children's fingers. We must not overreact to this new phenomenon or indeed shy away from it because it is sensitive, but rather take a common-sense approach to the issue. We do not want to alienate our children by making them feel shameful for being sexually curious, which is a normal part of a teenager's development. However, it is important that we monitor their internet usage and that we open up a dialogue about safe internet practices and explain to them the dangers of viewing sexually explicit images.

PORNOGRAPHY AND VIOLENCE

There is an absolute need for legislatures to protect our children from accessing extreme violent sexual imagery. In my experience, working in schools and as a psychotherapist, the earlier boys are exposed to such content, the more difficult it is for them to forge healthy, loving relationships. All the research is there illuminating the devastating impact pornography has on young minds. Not only does it dehumanise women but it also can lure vulnerable minds into a kind of fantasy world where sexual thoughts can metamorphose into dangerous sexual deviant behaviour. That's not to say that everyone who views such content will commit a violent act against women, but the research is quite clear: viewing pornography increases the potential for violence against women, dramatically. The terrible crimes that shook this country in recent years have left all of us feeling a little numb and confused. The senseless murder of a young girl at the hands of her classmates was as shocking as it was incomprehensible. And the abduction, rape and murder of a young Filipina woman at the hands of a stranger served as a chilling reminder of the evil that exists in the world. But we have to examine terrible events like these and ask the difficult questions: what confluence of events took place for something as heinous as those crimes to visit this island and those unfortunate girls? What happened to those perpetrators that they viewed these girls and women as prey? These are important questions to ask ourselves, as a society. It is easy to talk in terms of evil, but we have to look at extreme pornography and violent images that dehumanise women, and wonder what impact viewing those images has on a vulnerable mind. The easy access to extreme pornography is a dangerous new development in our children's life, and we have to protect them from it.

As soon as your child has a smartphone, they are only ever a few clicks from hardcore sexual imagery. We would not dream of letting our child wonder around the streets of any city without supervision, yet we remain supine while they roam around the far murkier and sinister landscape of the internet, where people can use avatars to hide their true identity and intentions. One of the many aspects that struck me about the 2018 sexual assault case in Northern Ireland was the language used by the defendants in their communications with each other. It was highly sexualised and graphic language that really could have only evolved from watching pornographic content. We need to look at this issue in our schools and start teaching young boys about the difference between extreme sexual material and intimate loving relationships. We also need to make it far more difficult for a child to access dangerous content.

Ted Bundy said before his execution for raping and killing over thirty women that in his experience of being incarcerated he had met a lot of men who were motivated to commit violence against women and, according to Bundy, 'without exception every one of them was deeply involved in pornography'. In that final interview he left a stark message for all parents and legislators: 'those of us who are influenced by pornographic violence are not inherently evil; we are your sons, husbands and brothers and pornography can reach out and snatch a child out of any house no matter how diligent the parents are.' While many might say that this was simply an excuse for abhorrent behaviour, and they may be right, the research shows us that exposure to violent sexual content can disrupt and corrupt vulnerable minds.

We know that viewing violent sexual content is damaging for our children. We know that such exposure greatly reduces true intimacy and negatively impacts on relationships. We know that pornography degrades and dehumanises women. So, why is it that we have not yet managed to come up with a sensible policy and make it much more difficult for children to view such material? We need to wake up and protect our children because the mobile phone companies are clearly not going to do it for us. We need to tackle the issue; we have to start the uncomfortable dialogue with our children about the difference between loving intimacy and extreme violent sexual content. We must also roll out initiatives in our schools to promote healthy smartphone usage. We can no longer say it is only a bit of harmless curiosity and a benign activity. It clearly is not. We must protect our sons and daughters by developing policies that make accessing graphic material far more difficult than it currently is. And by doing this we might finally help our children to develop healthy, loving relationships. Right now, it is down to us, the parents, to safeguard our children from these images. Of course, they should not be able to access them without age verification but that's not in place. So it falls on the parents. And we cannot look the other way while they are looking at extreme violent sexual content.

Case Study

Therese and John came to see me because they were having difficulties in their marriage. They were only married two years but things had become a little strained over recent months. This is taken from the third session. Therese did a lot of the talking in the early sessions. But here John opens up.

Richard: How have things been?
Therese: Things haven't been good between us.
Richard: Would you agree John?
John: Yeah, they haven't been great recently.
Richard: Can you describe what it has been like?
Therese: Well, John is irritable all the time. Nothing I do seems
  to be good enough and he just doesn't seem happy. We
  haven't been intimate in so long. We recently went on a
  holiday and it was a disaster, after all the money we spent.
Richard: Would you agree with that John?
John: Yeah.
Richard: Can I ask you to describe what it's like for you John,
  and could I ask you Therese to listen to John as if he is not

your husband but a stranger speaking about a different relationship?

Therese: Okay.

Richard: John, can you describe what things are like for you in the house?

John: I'm not really good at this sort of thing.

Richard: That's okay; take your time John. This is a judgement-free room. Whatever you are comfortable with; it's up to you.

John: Look, this is nothing to do with Therese. This is my problem that I need to figure out.

Richard: Do you want to say it here and we can all figure it out together?

John: I love Therese, more than anything. (Therese is crying.)

Richard: Thank you for sharing that.

John: I've always had an issue with pornography. (John is visibly uncomfortable.)

Richard: Okay, thank you for saying that here. You're not alone John. This is an issue affecting many couples in today's world.

John: I know it's not healthy but I can't stop looking at it. I hate myself for it. It's exhausting. I have to delete my history all the time; I'm viewing it on my phone in work. I know I need help. I really hate myself; that is why I'm so irritable, I know I have a problem. I can't stop. I tried; remember I got rid of my smartphone – that's because I wanted to get away from it. But then I started using the iPad. I hate myself. It's nothing to do with you Therese. It's me, I'm sick.

Richard: It sounds like you have really been struggling with this for some time John.

John: About twenty years. It's destroying me.

Richard: What's the worst thing viewing pornography has brought into your life?

John: It has taken Therese away from me. (John is very upset at this point.)

In this short case study we see the sheer pain and isolation something like pornography brings into a person's life. John had been labouring with the issue for a long time on his own. It had also impacted on his intimate relationship with his wife and it changed how he viewed himself. John was using pornography to satiate emotional distress. It really didn't take us long to break John's compulsion. He identified the stressors in his life and developed coping skills to manage them better. Once a teenager views pornographic material it can change what they expect from a sexual partner. This can have serious consequences when they start dating. In the following case study, Susan's story is a very familiar one in my work.

Case Study

Susan was fifteen years old when came to me because she started refusing to go to school. Her parents were worried about her because she had been a very sociable young girl. She had recently broken up with her boyfriend and her parents believed this was the cause of the change in her personality.

Richard: Can you tell me a little about why you are here today?
Susan: My parents are worried about me.
Richard: How do you know they are worried about you?
Susan: They tell me all the time, and they brought me here.
Richard: Did you want to come here?
Susan: I didn't mind.
Richard: Besides your parents being worried, is anyone else worried about you?
Susan: My grandmother. She says just beat him up.
Richard: Beat up who?
Susan: Cian.
Richard: Who is Cian?
Susan: The boy I was texting.
Richard: Dating?
Susan: Yeah.
Richard: Can you tell me a little about him?

Susan: Just a boy I thought I liked and I thought he liked me, but he didn't.
Richard: How do you know he doesn't like you?
Susan: I just do.
Richard: How did it end?
Susan: I didn't really even like him; I know that's what girls say when they get dumped but I didn't like him. All my friends were like 'you should meet him' and we were going to Wrights at Halloween so I met him that night and we started texting after that.
Richard: How long were you dating?
Susan: Two months.
Richard: Can you tell me how it ended?
Susan: Do you know Snapchat?
Richard: I do.
Susan: Well, one night after being in Wrights he asked me to send ... this is very embarrassing, I don't think I can say it.
Richard: You know Susan, there is very little that would shock me. This is a safe space for you to talk about anything you might want to look at.
Susan: Well, he had asked me before to send a picture of my chest. But I wouldn't. He sent me some of his, like chest and stomach, but I didn't ask for them. But he kept at me and that night I had drunk vodka and he asked again. This time he sent a pic of his, you know, and I sent one back of my chest. I don't know why I did, but he was my boyfriend and all my friends have done it. So I did. (Susan is crying now.)
Richard: It's okay Susan. What are your tears saying?
Susan: I'm ashamed; they are saying what a fool you are.
Richard: Why?
Susan: Because we broke up soon after and he has shown some of the boys in our group. Some of them have fought with him about it but I know some others have seen the picture and they are laughing when they see me. Or they are saying things in class like making a joke about me thinking I don't know. A teacher asked me a question in class and one of his

> friends said 'Susan can give you two good reasons for that.' And they all laughed. I knew what they meant.
> Richard: I'm sorry you have had this experience. But it will end soon, I can promise you that. Can I ask you a difficult question?
> Susan: Yeah.
> Richard: Have you thought about harming yourself?
> Susan: Yes.
> Richard: What have you thought about?
> Susan: That if I died they'd know how they hurt me. I could teach them a lesson.
> Richard: Did you think about how you would die?
> Susan: This will sound crazy, but I thought about cutting my wrists in class. But not seriously, I didn't plan it or anything. I just wanted to show them what they were doing to me.

This case study illuminates the awful predicament a young girl can find herself in if she sends an intimate image to someone else. This was a very interesting case because the boy in question had also been the victim of someone disseminating images of him. But we have to question where are these children getting the notion to send compromising images over their devices. Where are they picking up messages that normalise this kind of behaviour? In nearly all of the cases I have worked with, pornography is at the root of this sort of risky behaviour. As parents we have to minimise our children's contact with such images. In the case of John, his life had become intolerable because of his interest in pornography. It nearly cost him his marriage. And it had developed in his teenage years. In Susan's case she had become incredibly isolated and had even started to develop suicidal thoughts.

So our vigilance is crucial here. Obviously you can't check your child's phone all the time but you certainly can when they hand it over at night when you implement the no-technology-in-the-bedroom boundary. You might say 'but that's an invasion of their privacy'. But the teenage years are about creating your child's ability to be independent. I like to think of the teenage years as a holding autonomy;

they are not ready yet for full autonomy. In Chapter 6 I will discuss how to build your child's self-esteem because that is an important part of preventing your child from constantly looking for approval, which is often at the root of this issue.

6

Bullying

One of the most stressful events you can experience as a parent is to watch your child suffer at the hands of a bully. It can bring up so much for us: fear, anger and powerlessness are just some of the emotions we may feel. And our own childhood experiences are never too far from our interactions with our children. So it is very important, as parents, to support your child through such a difficult and challenging time as that of being bullied.

One of the first conversations I have with parents who come to my clinic because they are very concerned about their child's low mood and reluctance to go to school is around their child's self-esteem and levels of confidence. There is no doubt about it, a confident and self-assured child very rarely finds themselves being either the victim or perpetrator of bullying. Self-esteem is one of those rare and almost intangible things: it is nearly easier not to see than to see. I meet issues of low self-esteem in my clinic nearly every day. It can take many therapeutic conversations to erode those concrete negative ideas a child might hold about themselves. Often we receive or develop ideas about ourselves that are negative but we hold onto them because we believe them. I often utilise the metaphor of a puzzle for teenagers to elucidate how they have come to hold these damaging false narratives about themselves. I tell them that their internal puzzle has a certain shape and when they hear positive affirmation it doesn't fit with their puzzle, so it bounces off them and doesn't stick. However, when they hear a negative comment it slots right in because that's what they hold as a truth. Debunking that notion and unearthing where that voice took shape can help a child work on why they want to believe something so fundamentally negative about themselves.

What Can I Do as a Parent to Help My Child?

This is such an important question. A negative experience like bullying can be such a rich learning experience for your child. But your reaction will determine whether or not your child learns from it or collapses under it. Just remember, we all meet people in life who try to dominate us and take some power from us so developing the skills to handle this is hugely desirable for your child's successful future. As I said, it can be incredibly disturbing to think of our child out there being picked on by some other child. But we have to be a safe place when our child discloses a negative experience like bullying.

Tips on How to Help Your Bullied Child

- When your child tells you about the experience they are having, listen in a calm way. When a parent becomes agitated or angry about what they are hearing they are not supporting their child. They too are becoming victimised by the bully and are not supportive. The likelihood of your child telling you something in the future is diminished significantly when you over-react. Remember: be by their side, not on it.

- Teach your child some coping skills. Listen to the nature of the bullying. Obviously if it is physical you will need to report it to the school. But first, try to get your child to understand how to manage this negative experience. Bullying is about power and control. Often I hear children telling me 'I did what Mum said and I ignored him but it only got worse.' If you ignore the fact someone is calling you hurtful names you are giving them power over you. That is exactly what a child wants when they launch a hurtful or disparaging comment. Don't allow this to happen to your child. Teach them how to respond in a neutral way. I also hear children tell me, 'my dad says I should just knock him out or say something hurtful back' – both of these options are undesirable because they, more than likely, will escalate the issue. And that is the last thing you want to do as a parent. Let's just say they mock your child's shoes or haircut; role-play this with your child and teach them how to respond by saying something like 'yeah, good one' or 'whatever'. Responses like these are neutral and they ensure that you keep your power without escalating the situation.
- Explain to your child why someone would say a nasty, hurtful comment. Think of that puzzle I mentioned earlier: if a child has low self-esteem when they hear negative comments about themselves from their peer group they tend to internalise them and believe the reason they are receiving these comments is because they are worthless and weak. We must explain to our children that anyone who says something negative has a deep sadness in them, that's why they are launching such hurtful comments in the first place. I once had a conversation with a boy who had bullied a classmate; he told me, 'I guess I wanted him to feel how my dad made me feel.' This was a striking conversation and it illuminates why anyone would become the perpetrator of something as negative as bullying.

Self-Esteem

Re-building your child's self-esteem and confidence after being victimised by a bully is vitally important in helping them overcome such a negative experience. When you find yourself being targeted by someone it can really shake your fundamental understanding of yourself and, if not dealt with properly, it can last a lifetime. I often meet adults who come to my clinic looking for help because they have found themselves being targeted, once again, by someone in a very negative way in work. In those early conversations I am often introduced to that earlier child. I hear that voice so clearly: the sadness and isolation they experienced at the hands of a bully is very present in the room as they delineate this new experience of being bullied in work. They often talk about how they have allowed someone to position them in a particular way, or how that person must have seen something in them that promoted this subtle attack on them.

This kind of mindset illuminates just how destructive and negative bullying is on the psyche of the bullied. Why is it we are so quick to blame ourselves for someone else's behaviour? Remember that puzzle I utilised? Well if we have a negative view of ourselves or if we allow someone to print that view on our internal puzzle we will always struggle with self-esteem and confidence. And when we meet someone who says something negative about us we will believe them. Therefore, we come to view the behaviour of the bully as being provoked by something lacking in us. Nothing could be further from the truth. A bully targets someone for myriad reasons. And when we blame ourselves we hand over ultimate power to that person. That is not a desirable way to think about why you have been bullied. It certainly won't help you as you move forward into adult life and won't help you to recover your strength after an experience like being bullied. In fact, if you believe it was your fault you will constantly live in fear because you are waiting for someone else to spot that thing about you that made you a target in the first place.

A lot of the work I do in those early sessions is rewriting that script. Changing that narrative can be a difficult exercise because when you hold something as a truth about yourself, it can be uncomfortable and unsettling to see it as a falsehood. 'It must have been my fault, I'm weak' – I've heard this sentiment many times in my clinic. Challenging and changing that perception is a very significant endeavour if the person is to empower themselves after being bullied. And, as a parent, you must constantly work on building your child's self-esteem.

Tips on How to Rebuild Self-Esteem

- Explain to your child that it's not their fault. That might be a hard realisation to come to but it is an important one, because it is the truth. We so quickly blame ourselves for something that is entirely out of our control. But how you help your child to internalise it is in your control. Don't allow the bully any further head space in your child's mind.
- Help your child to understand that people become the target of bullies for many reasons. I talked with a young girl recently who was really labouring with what one of her friends had said to her. She told her that 'no one likes you because you're so stupid' and she was constantly making derogatory remarks about her clothes. When we unpacked where this negative behaviour was coming from, it didn't take us too long to figure out her friend was envious because she had recently started dating someone her friend had liked. You must explain to your child that when someone launches a negative comment or engages in persistent bullying behaviour there is something inside them that is unhappy or feels inadequate and they are trying to diminish your child to make themselves feel powerful. Understanding that takes a lot of their power away.
- Show your child how to journal their feelings; this is an important exercise for ameliorating the pain caused by bullying. Teach them how to work out those negative feelings through writing. This will help your child to rebuild their confidence.
- Your uniqueness is your strength. Teach your child to see themselves for how they truly are, not how they think others see them. We are all unique; celebrate that. Have a conversation about the fact that they were not targeted because they are

- unique but because someone else has an issue with who they themselves are.
- Try to find purpose from your child's experience. There is always something to be learned from every experience. What have they learned from their experience of being bullied? That they are strong enough to overcome it? That they will never allow anyone to take power from them again? That bullies are weak?

Being bullied and having someone target you in a negative way can erode your child's self-esteem. However, how you help your child to come to understand that experience will either empower your child or continue to make them see themselves as a victim. Choose to be powerful. Help your child to regain their strength once again.

WHAT HAPPENS WHEN YOUR CHILD IS THE BULLY?

It can be very unsettling to receive a call from the school to inform you that your child has been involved in targeting another student in a very negative way. While your immediate reaction may be to defend your child and deny that they would ever be involved in anything like bullying, your reaction to the information you are given is very important if your child is going to learn how to stop this negative behaviour. Children bully for many reasons. Children are not born bullies; children learn how to bully, so it is vitally important that you think about where your child might have picked up this maladaptive behaviour. This is not about blame but rather trying to ascertain why your child has such a low level of empathy that they are willing to subject another child to bullying. A considerable amount of the work I do in schools is helping the management team draft a sensible bullying policy. The last thing anyone wants to do is to further exacerbate the issue with an over-the-top reaction to something that requires a sensitive and delicate approach. And the school can really come under extreme pressure to deal with the issue in a particular way that might not be in the best interests of all involved. Understanding how the bullying started and the nature of what is taking place are two very important aspects of making sure it does not continue.

What to Do if Your Child Is the Bully

- When you receive the information from the school control your response. Do not overreact; instead be calm and think of how your child might have developed this behaviour. The majority of children who bully are struggling with issues themselves. Try to discover what is it that your child is dealing with. They haven't always behaved like this – so what has changed? If you simply discipline your child, you may stop the behaviour but you haven't discovered the root causes of this issue and therefore it may rise again. Get to the root cause of the issue: self-esteem, power, control.
- Listen to your child's explanation in a supportive way, but also let them know that bullying is never an acceptable way to deal with a personal issue. Develop their sense of empathy. To engage in bullying illuminates that their sense of empathy may need addressing. I had a conversation with a student recently who had been saying very nasty stuff to another boy in his class. And when I asked him to describe how the other student might feel he struggled to do so. It was clear that empathy was lacking for this boy and therefore he didn't have any problem launching such hurtful and devastating comments. Get them to describe what it must be like for the person on the other end of those comments.
- Support the school's disciplinary action. It is incredibly important that your child sees just how united the school and their family are against bullying. When parents fight with the school or do not engage with the disciplinary process they are losing the opportunity to teach their child such an important lesson about life. When a family blames the school they are showing their child that you never fully take responsibility for your behaviour, and that is one of the crucial learning points if you are to ameliorate this negative behaviour. Show them that all behaviours have consequences.
- Reinforce positive behaviour. Often children bully for attention, whether that is from their peer group or teachers. Make sure

they are getting the attention they need from positive behaviour. I had a student explain to me last year when I talked to him about his behaviour, 'at least when I'm aggressive people pay attention to me.' It is important that our children receive positive feedback when they do something worthy of it. We all crave attention – make sure your child is getting that attention in a healthy way.

It is not helpful to think of the child who is bullying as a monster. Sometimes the victim of bullying can go on to become the perpetrator of bullying. Supporting our children in a way that allows them to grow from their mistakes and holding them while they navigate the difficult landscape of the teenage world is a major part of our duty as parents. When we learn that our child is victimising another we must work with the school to support our child so that they learn how to better represent themselves in the world.

* * *

Bullying is a very challenging experience for everyone. But, as parents, we must remain calm when our child tells us about their experience. I find doing something I call 'bullying lessons' with my own children very helpful. I go through different scenarios of what bullies might say and then I unpack the context to that behaviour. In fact, my eldest daughter experienced something negative in school recently but because of those lessons she understood why someone would say something mean to another child. This took all the power out of the encounter. Helping our children to understand why people say the things they do helps them enormously to navigate those early relational dynamics. Your child, more than likely, will experience some form of bullying over the course of their formative years. How you react and talk to them through those encounters will determine whether or not your child learns how to cope with them and will instil in them a sense of self-worth and confidence that will deter any future bully.

7

Cyberbullying

CYBERBULLYING: AN INCREASING CHALLENGE FOR PARENTS AND SCHOOLS

What was traditionally confined to the school environment has now, with the proliferation of electronic media, become a potentially ubiquitous occurrence for children and teenagers alike. Cyberbullying is defined as any behaviour performed through electronic or digital media by individuals or groups that repeatedly communicates hostile or aggressive messages intended to inflict harm or discomfort on others. This can include harassment via text or picture/video messages, in online games, on websites and social networking sites, in chatrooms, or via email or Twitter; it can take the form of posting abusive comments on blogs or harassment in virtual environments; and it can make the receiver of these hurtful messages feel like they have no way out of the situation. What makes this type of bullying so dangerous to the well-being of our children is the fact that the victims of cyberbullying are never beyond the reach of their harassers. We are surrounded by the terrifying stories of so many children who have taken their own lives in a terrible and drastic attempt to stop the abusive online comments.

Early intervention is crucial here to protect our children from this type of modern-day bullying. Parents need to understand how to best support their child going through an experience as devastating as cyberbullying. Schools and parents need to also educate children on the hurt caused when something negative gets posted online. In my experience working with the perpetrators of cyberbullying, they often do not realise the extent of the harm they are causing with their words and actions. Talking to your child about their online activity and looking at the content they are posting will help to protect them from becoming a victim or a perpetrator of such a crime. Another feature of cyberbullying that I have often encountered is a child's reticence to report their experience in the first place. They believe the school will not handle the issue correctly or sensitively and that they will be seen to be telling on their classmates and this will further increase the negative interactions online. So they get caught in a bind – whom do they tell? And often they don't tell their parents because they think they will contact the school and that, as I said, will only make things worse. Also many of the children I deal with are very embarrassed about what is happening to them, so this is an incredibly isolating experience for the victim and they often feel like they have no one to turn to, which is a very dangerous mindset for a child to be in.

We have far too many stories in our society about young adults becoming victimsed through social media not to pay it attention. As parents, we must help our children translate what is happening to them. And cyberbulling can be a very scary experience for a child to go through because they are never free from the reach of the bully. You have to consider the possibility of cyberbullying if you notice a dramatic and severe dip in your child's mental state. Because, as I said, there are many reasons why they will not tell you about what is going on for them and a child can think that suicide is a viable option to alleviate a present negative experience without really understanding the absolute permanence of that decision.

Research highlights that the majority of cyberbullying occurs between the ages of ten and fourteen years. Because of the extreme importance of peer relations and social acceptance in this age group, cyberbullying can be a particularly devastating experience for a child. Unlike face-to-face bullying, which typically happens within the school milieu and is generally witnessed by others and is carried out by a perpetrator who is known to or seen by the victim, messages posted online can be spread globally and can exist in perpetuity, and the perpetrator can conceal their identity by using an avatar. The trouble with developing a school policy that adequately deals with this serious issue is the fact that these virtual forums are constantly changing. So when an issue arises, what parents often find is that the school policy, which was drafted to solve a previous case, is no longer fit for purpose. Furthermore, such policies in schools have focused primarily on punishing the cyberbully rather than on developing holistic solutions that cultivate more respectful online exchanges and build a more empathetic culture within our schools. What we need to do as parents and teachers is to teach our children how to make the right decisions that keep them safe online when we are not watching.

The rapid advancement of smartphones and internet technologies has opened up new vistas and infinite spaces that young people can explore with fewer restrictions. Not all of this new virtual landscape is negative – on the contrary, there is a myriad of educational benefits to these new and exciting avenues of learning. However, the reality remains that for the most part our children are navigating these worlds with very little parental supervision.

In recent years I have been struck by the sheer magnitude of cyberbullying which was taking place through gaming. The Xbox, in particular, has been a hot bed of subtle, covert cyberbullying. And it has proven very difficult for both parents and schools to manage. In my practice I met a young teenager who had contemplated suicide because he believed he had no way out of the situation he found himself in. The most troubling aspect of his story was the fact that while his parents believed he was safe in his room studying, he was in fact being tormented by a group of his peers online. Feelings of isolation and having nowhere to turn led him to contemplate taking his own life. When I asked him to describe his experience he said, 'I felt I had no choice but to kill myself; I just wanted it to stop, it felt like I couldn't get away from them.' These words are a chilling reminder of the feelings experienced by our children when they are being targeted online. While traditional bullying and cyberbullying have many commonalities, the main difference is that cyberbullying means that no space in the teenager's world is safe from the reach of negative feedback.

What Can I Do if My Child Is Being Bullied Online?

- Your reaction is very important. While it can be very distressing to think of your child being tormented by an unknown group or person online, if you become angry you are telling your child that they should be very worried. This will only further increase the levels of anxiety your child is experiencing.
- You must not ban your child from their devices. If you do this, the chances are they will never confide in you again. And you will further increase their sense of alienation.
- Calmly listen to your child and be supportive while they describe their experience.
- Thank them for coming to you and acknowledge that it takes a lot of courage for them to talk about an issue like this.
- Learn how to block and report other profiles on sites like Facebook and Twitter.
- Make sure they do not respond to the message or comment. While your first reaction maybe to send a message back, this only feeds the problem. The worst thing that can happen to a troll or cyberbully is silence.
- Record the message if it is possible.
- Restrict your child's privacy settings on Facebook and other social media sites to 'friends only', protect their tweets, hide their profile from the Facebook search engine, and disable

'anonymous' questions in the settings on the various platforms your child may be accessing.
- Contact the school and explain your child's experience calmly and work with the school to resolve the situation. Try not to blame the school; your reaction is very important for a successful outcome with this issue. If you are likely to overreact, be confrontational or blame the school, the chances are your child will not confide in you in the first place. We have to show our children that we are a safe place to come to when they have an issue.
- If it persists contact the Gardaí. It is illegal to disseminate hateful content online.

In spite of the challenges that parents face in monitoring their adolescents' online experiences, research clearly shows that parents who are supportive and monitor their child's internet usage significantly decrease the chances of their child becoming a victim or perpetrator of cyberbullying.

Case Study

The Halloran family came to my clinic after their son had experienced online bullying. The entire family attended the sessions: Mother (Patricia), Father (David), Michael, the boy who had been bullied (16), Sebastian (14) and Lily (8). This is a collection of different conversations we had over a twelve-week period.

Richard: Can you describe how it started, Michael?
Michael: We were playing football at lunch with a tennis ball and my friend kicked the ball and it hit me in the face; it was really sore and the teacher saw it and came over and gave out to Alan and I went into the toilet because I was crying and didn't want them to see. The next day when I tried to join the game again they said things like, 'no one wants you to play, you might get hurt' and that sort of thing. And it developed from there. The name-calling got worse and they

started to avoid me and run when I came over and then they started saying things about me online and on the games.

Richard: That sounds like a very difficult time. Did you have anyone you could talk to about this?

Michael: No, not really.

Patricia: I noticed he didn't want to go to school, but he wouldn't say why when I asked.

David: We did ask.

Richard: What did you feel would happen if you told someone?

Michael: It would get worse; I knew I couldn't tell Mum because she'd tell the school and Dad would only say I should be stronger, or toughen up.

David: I wouldn't have said that.

Michael: What about the time when that boy hit me at the match and you gave out to me in the car on the way home about not standing up for myself.

David: I was just trying to say don't let someone hit you. That's all.

Michael: And when you saw a message on Xbox what did you do?

David: I told them to F off. What's wrong with that?

Michael: You don't have to go to school with them.

David: You have to stand up to bullies; the only thing they respect is a good slap.

Patricia: Stop David.

Richard: When did things get worse?

Michael: When I told Mum.

Patricia: I went to the school about it and they told me they would deal with it.

Michael: It made it way worse. And they saw you in the school and they knew I had told you and now, you know what, they are calling me 'rat' on top of everything else.

Sebastian: I've heard them on the bus, shouting that.

Richard: How does that make you feel, Sebastian?

Sebastian: I want to hit them. He's not a rat.

Michael: Thanks Sebastian.

David: I don't understand why the school won't do anything; we've told them about it over and over again. It has been so stressful for us all.
Patricia: Our relationship with the school isn't good now – what did you call the principal?
David: Come on, Patricia. I know.
Patricia: Go on, what did you call him?
David: What's the point in that now? Trying to humiliate me in front of Richard.
Richard: I understand that this is very stressful for everyone, and it's very difficult to watch your son receive this kind of treatment from his peer group. No one is judging here. And I don't know how I would react if my daughter had an experience like this but in my professional experience certain approaches are more helpful than others.
Richard: Can I just ask Michael, what were the worst thoughts you had when you thought about all of this?
Michael: I didn't know how to stop it all. I lost my friends. I had no one. I just wanted to stay under the covers and never come out.
Richard: Do you have any other friends in school?
Patricia: He has Tom, you like him – don't you?
Michael: Yeah.
Richard: If I had a magic wand what would you change?
Michael: I wouldn't cry when the ball hit me.
Richard: Would you change anything else?
Michael: Make them my friends again.

You can see from this conversation how complicated cyberbullying is and how our reaction to it can help or further increase a child's sense of alienation. Cyberbullying is a very insidious thing because often the person victimising someone is not even aware that they are doing anything wrong. It is normal to fall out with your friends over the course of adolescence but with technology and smartphones it means that children have the potential to launch very hurtful and permanent comments about a friend in the heat of the moment.

And children do not, for the most part, understand the pain it can cause to the recipient.

In the case study above there were a number of things that the parents could have done to ensure a more effective approach to the issue. Firstly, the father's reaction to bullies was slightly misguided and archaic. Many children are not physical and to tell your child to be physical with a bully is only going to create a further decrease in their self-esteem. When told to fight back a child can see that as just another aspect of their personality that is weak. So, try to avoid promoting violence. And think of it this way – let's say your son does go into school and punches the bully, what happens now? Best-case scenario he beats the bully up, which really isn't a best-case scenario at all. He could be sued or, worse, he could injure the boy. So telling your child they should 'deal with it like a man' isn't a sensible approach in today's world.

While most fathers probably deep down want their son to be strong and physically respected by his peer group, not all children are like that and we must respect the individuality of each child we have in front of us. Michael was not a physical child at all. So telling him to defend himself was placing more stress on him. Boys crave the respect of their fathers; therefore it is important that the father understands how to best support his child in an issue like cyberbullying. Also the father's engagement with the school was very negative. It was obvious that he felt powerless in the situation and had reverted to a childish way of dealing with the issue. You could argue that he had become the bully and was subjecting the principal to the very behaviour he wanted him to protect his son from. I work in schools and I see this frequently; it really does not motivate the school system in your favour. You have to work with the school and have a healthy joint systems approach to the issue if there is going to be a successful outcome.

It was obvious why Michael didn't inform his parents immediately when the issue was developing. He knew what their reaction was going to be. They were not going to listen to him, and were only going to heighten his sense of stress, which proved the case when he eventually did confide in them. We have to show our children that we are a safe space when they need someone to talk to. If we over-react and do not listen to them, they will learn not to seek our advice when they are in trouble. This can prove detrimental to the safety and well-being of your child. Ask yourself:

- How do I react when my child has an issue?
- Whose needs am I meeting with that reaction?
- How can I better support my child when they need me?

Task

The next time your child comes to you with a difficulty, try to remain unemotional. Place yourself in a supporting role. Listen and avoid lecturing. Tell them what you would do in that situation. Jot down your child's reaction to your reaction. Notice has anything changed. Make a note of it. The most dangerous aspect of this type of bullying is that it can make a child feel completely alone, embarrassed and trapped. By providing them with supportive parenting you will become that safe place they need to vent when they are going through a problem in their social world. And the chances are, the rupture in peer relations that caused the issue will more than likely be forgotten about and they will be friends again, and you haven't rushed in to judge their friends or label them with name-calling. You have truly supported your child.

… 8 …

Modern Approaches to Teenage Anxiety

One of the most prevalent issues I encounter in the therapeutic setting is that of teenage anxiety. It can take the shape of many forms, from social anxiety to school refusal to general feelings of not wanting to go outside to a complete paralysis due to excessive worrying or ritualistic behaviours. Living with a child who is suffering with anxiety can be a very challenging experience for the entire family unit. Parents often come to therapy in a last-ditch effort to alleviate the strain the entire family has been labouring under as a result of their child's anxiety. In this chapter I am going to explore how you can support a child who is anxious and how you can build your child's resilience so that they have the skills to deal with an anxiety-provoking situation without it completely overwhelming them.

Over the years, I have been struck by the sheer number of students suffering with anxiety in the classroom. Often, it isn't until the parent–teacher meeting that the full extent of the issue is revealed, which means that, for the most part, the child has been suffering in silence for fear of being exposed. However, sometimes it is so blatantly apparent because the student has lumps of hair missing on their head. Trichotillomania, the pulling out of hair, for many teachers and students alike can be a disturbing experience in the classroom. But it is far more common than we would like to think. And often it is not as severe as it looks. In my experience many students get caught satiating their anxiety by turning their hair repeatedly. This friction can cause the hair to fall out, so it's not like the child is literally pulling their hair out, but it is more that the soothing repetitiveness of spinning the hair around their finger causes the hair to fall out. Often simply replacing the hair twirling with something else soothing can solve the issue of trichotillomania.

How we react to our child's anxiety is incredibly important for a successful outcome. And remember anxiety is not all bad. We will all feel anxious at times and often that anxiety can help us to excel, so it's about understanding how to cope with it and harness it to our favour.

The Reframing of Anxiety

Anxiety has its place. Sports stars will often talk about how they need a certain amount of it before any big performance. Personally, when I was younger, if I didn't feel somewhat anxious before a university exam I would be worried that perhaps I wasn't prepared enough. I felt I needed a degree of anxiety to perform at a high level. So, not all anxiety is bad. Research shows that when you fear something and your anxiety is in the extreme, however, it will inevitably impact you in a negative way. By understanding anxiety and how not all anxiety is bad, we can start to support our children fully. Let's just say you have a fear of heights and in an exercise to show you how your fear can bring about the very thing you are fearful of, I ask you to walk on a plank a foot off the ground. You can do it with ease, no problem. Now let's say I move that very same plank ten feet into the air, what will happen now? Well, more than likely you will fall because you are fearful of falling and this fear will make you apprehensive and clumsy, and ultimately help you to bring into being the self-fulfilling prophesy that you hold so deeply: heights are dangerous. Of course heights can be dangerous, but what about the trapeze artist? How would they navigate the plank? Well, they would probably do handstands on it, smiling. What is the difference between you and the circus performer? Well, competency, yes. But what creates that competency? Ultimately it's down to how you view heights and the fundamental belief you hold about yourself.

The same mentality is important for understanding your child's anxiety. If you change how they view themselves and their anxiety you will change their relationship with it. Anxiety does not destroy us; it does not have to be something we fear. Anxiety will come into your life and anxiety will leave your life. It is not a permanent state. And the difference between a child who can manage their anxiety and a child who cannot is having this understanding. Children who cannot manage anxiety speak in absolutes and are pessimistic in their outlook – 'I will never get over this', 'I will always be anxious' – whereas a child who can cope with anxiety is more positive in their outlook and will say 'it will pass', 'I'm not always anxious'. Remember you cannot defeat anxiety, we are hardwired to experience it; we must learn how to hear it and use it to our benefit.

Often, I encounter teenagers who are caught in an illogical fear or phobia. They really do not have any insight into what has caused this fear. In some cases they may not even know what the fear is; they just know it's there. When I'm confronted with an illogical fear, I'm often reminded of the story of the woman who has a phobia of elephants. Every day she anxiously prays that elephants will not trample her and every day nothing happens. When her neighbour explains that she lives in England, where there are no elephants, she replies, 'you see, my prayers work.' I often find that teenagers can get themselves caught in an illogical way of thinking, like this woman. But for them, it becomes logical. They subconsciously develop the belief that the more they worry the more they are protected from bad things happening. So they do not really understand why they are worrying and they can be very confused about it. Breaking this belief can be a significant step in overcoming anxiety in teenagers.

Teenagers often come to me with very strong or concrete narratives about themselves. The family or the school system often hands down these narratives to the child. They can become entrenched or fixed and may be difficult to move. The child comes to view themselves as 'worriers'. I find trying to re-author these narratives is a very important part of the work I do with families experiencing a child who is anxious. And it is important, as a parent, that you do not label your child as anxious or a worrier. The purpose of a label is not to predict the future but to tell it. So, if you label your child as a nervous child, that's exactly what they will become. For example, I had a family come to see me some time ago because their youngest daughter was very anxious. She was ruminating on thoughts of her parents' death and had developed a fear of going outside. So much so that she wouldn't let her mother leave her side for fear the mother would be killed in a car crash. This was placing huge strain on the entire family unit. When I asked her what she was experiencing she described very painfully the fear of her parents' death. It was striking how vivid and real this was for her. Her parents also delineated how she was always an anxious child. When I asked her to describe a time when she wasn't anxious, her whole demeanour shifted. She warmly recalled a trip to Disneyland when she was eight years old. When I pointed out for the family that she wasn't always anxious, the daughter became visibly lighter. Maybe this identity wasn't fixed. Maybe it was transient, and maybe anxiety came into her life and maybe it would also leave her life again.

It is very important that we don't hand down negative narratives about our children. I often hear parents say, 'he is just like his grandfather; he was very anxious too.' Nothing will make your child more anxious than hearing a narrative like this. They will feel powerless to it and almost have to live it out to please the narrative. And parents are often unconscious of the messages they are giving their children and the narrative they are writing for them.

In the conversation mentioned above I was attempting to remove the rigidity of the girl's identity as being an 'anxious child'.

She wasn't always anxious. I was re-authoring her story, bringing old sub-narratives, lost to the dominant one about anxiety, back into prominence in the girl's life. In fact, in a later session it became clear that the girl's anxiety was present because she felt it was holding the family together. While her mother and father were focused on her they were not focused on the problems in their relationship, which the child had picked up on. So her illogical fear, when viewed this way, was very logical. Often parents talk in terms of 'how did we get here?' 'How is my child so anxious?' This places the locus of the problem intrapsychic (within) the child. However, in my experience, a child's anxiety has more to do with the system or ecology they are navigating than anything inherently pathological inside them.

Anxiety impacts us all at times. Our children will experience bouts of it over the course of their young lives. As parents we must learn to teach our children coping strategies, and not to label them as 'anxious children'. When we give a child a negative label we are not predicting the future, we are writing it. Keep that in mind the next time you think of your child in those kinds of terms and remember anxiety is not fixed, it comes and goes. Parents often come to me feeling they have exhausted every avenue and are looking for practical steps to help their child's anxiety. These parents often present as being very anxious themselves. When parents ask me 'so what should we do?' I begin by looking at what has been their approach so far. It's important, in the early stages, to identify what hasn't worked. Often the parents' efforts have added to the sense of stress and anxiety in the house. So, in this chapter I'm going to outline three easy steps to follow to help your child deal with anxiety.

The following information is very important for parents to consider before they attempt to help their child cope with anxiety. Stop trying to help your child to get rid of anxiety. This is not a helpful way to view the issue. As I said, anxiety is a part of us all. And we will all feel varying degrees of anxiety as we go through our lives. You must help your child to cope with it when it does arise. This is the first important step. Change how you view anxiety. Telling your child you are going to help them get rid of it is just setting your child up for future failure and will add to their low self-esteem. Anxiety is another thing they fail at.

The number of times I hear parents telling their child 'we will fight this together'; that language is very combative and ultimately unhelpful because we cannot defeat anxiety like it is an invading army, but we can certainly learn how to manage it. So, think in terms of helping your child to cope with anxiety when it does appear. That way your child isn't fearful of it returning. Remember also what I said about what happens when you fear something – inevitably that fear will bring the very thing you are nervous about into life. The reality is, the anxiety will return, but you will have taught your child clear strategies to manage that sudden wave of panic that can accompany those initial feelings of anxiousness. That is why I ask parents about their efforts so far because changing this view is massively significant if there is to be a positive outcome for the anxious child.

THREE EASY STEPS TO HELP YOUR CHILD COPE WITH ANXIETY

1. Try to avoid joining your child in their worry. Listen to them and try to understand what it is they are fearful of but do not allow this to become all-consuming. When every conversation is about the worry you are making it a dominant narrative and implicitly telling your child that they should be worried. Allocate a time for a discussion on it and then try not to talk about it again until the next allotted time. Remember: *be by their side, not on it*. When you join them in their sense of panic you are reinforcing the fact that they should be anxious.
2. Ask yourself, where did my child learn this negative reaction to a perceived adverse stimulus? Am I modelling how you should cope with anxiety? Show your child a positive way to deal with anxiety. Talk through their feelings and give them ways to deal with those feelings. But remember tip one – do not spend an inordinate amount of time on it. Just explain what they should do, like taking time to allow the feelings to dissipate or taking a breath or remembering to say 'this will pass. I will feel good again.' Role-play it for them so they can clearly see how someone deals with anxiety. Remember,

you're not teaching them to defeat anxiety but rather how to cope with it.
3. Do not try to take on too much too soon. Remember this: too much difference is dangerous for a child. If they have a fear of going out into big open spaces make sure you start by going out into small spaces that are manageable. Parents often have the idea that if they just put their child into a big space that will cure them. Like the child who is fearful of water and you just throw them in. That is not going to cure the issue: in fact it is only going to further exacerbate that sense of fear. That child will never go near water again because you have just illustrated that their fear was real. Your approach should be step by step. Don't push too much too soon. And don't make a big issue about going out somewhere that might be a little crowded. For example, if your child is having an issue with school refusal you could compromise with them by saying 'ok, you can go in for the morning but if you're not comfortable then I will collect you after lunch.' Or 'how about we do every second day this week?' This way you are slowly breaking the fear step by step.

Remember it is not about beating anxiety but rather instilling in your child coping mechanisms that will allow them to successfully manage a bout of anxiety when it does inevitably occur. We cannot remove anxiety from our children. But, as parents, we can teach them that feelings of anxiety are transient and they will pass and they are actually quite manageable.

ANXIETY AND SCHOOL REFUSAL

Usually around three weeks into the new school term, most children have gotten over that initial negative reaction that 'back to school' brings in its wake and the family have generally settled into the new rhythm of school life. While this may be the case for most families, there are a growing number of children for whom the notion of going back to school has become a deeply traumatic event. For parents confronted with school refusal, it can be a very stressful and confusing time as they are left desperately trying to understand what it is their child is going through and what best they can do to help ease their child's transition back into the school system.

There are many reasons why a child may refuse to attend school. Understanding the behaviour and what it is saying to us is paramount if there is to be a successful outcome. Some of the reasons for school refusal may be originating within the ecology of the school, such as:

- Social and peer-related difficulties
- Learning and curriculum difficulties
- Notions of perfectionism
- Difficulties with the physical environment

Other reasons may be rooted in the family system, such as:

- Marital issues
- Home may be more attractive than school
- Attention-receiving behaviour
- Parental inconsistencies

Early identification of causes of the behaviour is a key factor in developing appropriate strategies and interventions that the school, class teachers and parents can adopt. Parents can often, at times, feel very ashamed about their child's opposition to school. However, research shows that the longer a child refuses to attend school the more entrenched the child becomes in the behaviour, which makes breaking the pattern of refusal more problematic for all concerned. So, early intervention is critical. And it is nothing to be ashamed of; the majority of children at some point in their education develop an issue with school attendance. But the prognosis is very good, and for most children it is a brief, transient issue in their long, healthy educational life.

I met a family who came into therapy because their young adolescent daughter was refusing to go to school. The urgency the family felt to get their child back into the school system was very much in the room. If a child under sixteen years of age misses more

Thoughts that lead to refusal:

1. I can't leave home, something bad will happen if I'm not there. No one can laugh at me at home. No one will find out I'm not perfect when I'm at home. Mum/Dad will spend more time with me. I don't have to face the bully at home. Home is where all my computer games are. Home is much better than school. I hate yard time.

2. Once the behaviour progress this impacts on thoughts and these initial thoughts give way to thoughts far more devastating for a young person's psyche, like: 'I can't go in now, I've been out so long. Everyone will be talking about me. No one will want to play with me. They will think I am weird. So, I must be weird. I'm never going back there again.'

Behaviour:

1. Refusal to get ready for school. Refusal to attend school. Crying. Tantrums. Avoidance of any school-based situations. Fighting.

2. The behaviour now becomes entrenched. The child is stuck and does not know how to escape the cycle. The behaviour seems unbreakable. Malingering is a common behaviour at this stage.

Feelings that arise from having these kind of thoughts:

1. Anxiety, fear/pleasure, sadness, uncertainty, insecurity, overwhelmed.

2. These feelings change to embarrassment, inferiority, shame and isolation.

than twenty days the school must inform the statutory Educational Welfare Services. The parents were cognisant of this and so they were extremely eager to get their daughter back into school before they had to engage with this agency. In one of our conversations, the girls disclosed to me that when she was in school she couldn't help her parents. The child felt that if she stayed at home she could prevent her parents from fighting and therefore keep them from separating. Her story was strikingly similar to the previous girl's story, where she felt her anxiety was keeping her parents focused on her and not on each other. The source of your child's anxiety can be a very complicated and difficult thing to understand. However, in this case her school refusal, which was designed to save the family from disintegrating, was in fact placing more pressure on her parents. She found herself caught in a very complex cycle – that which was designed to elevate parental distress was in fact creating it. When I pointed out this pattern to her, her school refusal ended.

The diagram on page 93 shows the patterns to be aware of.

What Should Parents Do?

Parents, in their desperation to solve the issue, can at times further exasperate the problem. For example, recently I came across a mother at the school gate consoling her crying child. I listened as the mother frantically reassured her child. The child's sobbing only grew worse as each new reassuring word landed in his eardrum. Eventually, the parent turned away with the child and left the school. I could feel her frustration and despair, because I have been there myself with my own daughter. Mike Tyson once said that 'everyone has a plan until they get punched in the face', and when my own child started crying hysterically all the theory I had almost disappeared. More recently, my daughter changed school. We were concerned because she had loved the school she was in and had made really lovely friends but we had moved area and it wasn't feasible to keep her in the school anymore, so she had to move. A few days before she started in her new school my wife asked me could I take the morning off and go with them for her first day of her new school. So I thought about it. As I analysed it, I wondered what message would I be giving my daughter if I was suddenly there with her walking into school and whose needs would I be meeting by doing that? So I decided against it, and let her go to school like she normally does with my wife. Of course I wanted to go with her and share that special day in her educational journey, but I felt she would sense what my presence meant and become anxious herself. The way we react in these situations is crucial to a positive outcome. We have to be careful of the way we communicate to our children. If a child avoids an anxiety-provoking situation their anxiety subsides without learning that by staying in that situation the anxiety will eventually decrease of its own accord. In the situation above with the parent at the gates of the school, the parent was telling the child 'everything is going to be alright' but her body language was saying something else; the child was picking up on this inconsistency and it was further increasing the child's sense of anxiety and fear. A question I often ask myself when analysing school refusal is 'what is the underlining feeling here?' Normally, parents will say 'fear' but in many cases it is pleasure:

- More time with Mum
- Playing my computer games more
- More attention, family is rallying around this behaviour, it seems powerful
- I have a voice now

When I feel that school refusal is pleasure-driven, I inform the parents to take all the rewards out of the child staying at home. I instruct them to remove all computer games, TV, phones, etc. By making the day as dull as possible school becomes more attractive.

Nearly every child at some point in their educational career develops feelings of anxiety about their school environment. While for most students these feelings are transient and dissipate over time, for other students, however, these feelings develop into long-term school refusal. It is vital that parents communicate with the school when difficulties emerge so that the school and the family are united in an intervention that best suits their child.

Tips for Dealing with Your Child's Refusal to Attend School:

1. Stay calm. While it can be very stressful to watch your child go through an issue like school refusal, you must remain clam. If you become anxious and stressed about the situation you will be communicating to your child that their anxiety is well-founded and this will further exacerbate the situation. So, just listen to their concerns in a very controlled and non-emotional way. If you do this, you will be able to support them without adding to their stress. Remember: be by your child's side, not on it.
2. Talk to the school. There will need to be a joint approach to this issue if it is to be successful. A teacher will add another lens to the issue and help you to work towards a strategy. If there is not a strain in peer relations and if the school milieu is not the issue, this will help you in your approach. Maybe it's an attachment issue or maybe home life is too appealing. Through your discussions with the school and your child's teacher you will be able to narrow down the root cause of the issue.
3. Try to avoid allowing your child stay home. Even if it's for an hour, try to get your child to attend school. The more they are allowed to stay home the more the behaviour becomes entrenched and difficult to break. I know it can be very unsettling when you are confronted with a child who is nauseous or crying but when you give into your child's demands to stay home you're reinforcing avoidance and this is not desirable at all. So reaching a compromise will be important in the early stages of this issue. Say something like, 'if you go in for an hour and you still feel the same you can go to the office and they will ring me.' Often, we fear the idea of something more than the reality – so by allowing your child to stay at home you are feeding that fear and this will increase their dread of school. They come to think that they have been out so long that everyone now will be talking about them. This is a destructive mindset and it makes returning to school nearly impossible

for the child. So, by making them attend even for a class or for a half an hour you are taking away the potential for those feelings to develop.
4. Have a boundary around technology. Remove all games and devices from the bedroom. I have noticed over recent years that more and more children are presenting with school refusal because they are just simply tired after staying up all night playing their games. So, they get into a negative pattern of playing games through the night and staying in bed all day. Make sure that is not happening. Make the bedroom as unappealing as possible.
5. Be authoritative, not authoritarian. Keep your plan simple. Have a strategy to make home life like school. If they refuse to go into school clearly explain to them that they will still have to do the schoolwork. Let them know that you will be in contact with the school and that you will be bringing in their homework the following day. Make sure the work is corrected and positive reinforcement is applied. This way you are making going back to school more appealing. It really is about breaking the cycle of absence. Children dread going in the longer they are out. And if you keep the connection with the school going you will make breaking that cycle much easier for your child.

Understanding School Refusal

In my experience a child's reluctance to go to school can really test both the school and family as these joint systems try to develop effective strategies to get the child back into the classroom. However, it often fails because they view the locus of the issue as emanating only from within the child. And school refusal can be far more complicated than that. As I said, most children at some point in their educational career will try to avoid attending school. Often it is fleeting and does not need outside help. However, when a child develops what seems to the ordinary eye to be an irrational fear of school, parents can be left confused and unsure of what to do. So what is school refusal? It is important not to confuse truancy with school refusal. Truancy is the activity of not going to school because the student has discovered something better to do like hanging out with their friends at the amusement park or going to the beach. It's not so much that they fear school but rather they have something more exciting to do. School refusal can come from a far more complicated and darker psychological place. School refusal is generally the avoidance of the school environment due to the stress that environment places on the psyche of the child. Children who avoid school consistently normally do so because:

- The child wants to escape from situations that cause them distress, like the canteen, lunch, traveling to school by bus or train, or a particular teacher or class.
- Performance anxiety – the modern classroom is a far more active and demanding place than ever before and children are expected to offer opinions in the classroom. This can be quite daunting for a child who is suffering with anxiety or is naturally more introverted, so they avoid the situation altogether.
- Attachment disorder – spending more time at home allows them time with a parent they do not want to leave.
- Strained peer relations – often when a child suddenly develops an aversion to the school milieu they have suffered a fracture in their peer relations. Understanding this is an important step to a successful outcome.
- Spending more time in the bedroom – the arrival of technology and ubiquitous internet means the bedroom is a far more attractive place because they can play games like *Fortnite* for as long as they want.

From these examples you can see that in only two cases the problem is coming from within the child. So understanding the origin of the issue is very important if there is to be a desirable outcome. All behaviour is communication, so ask yourself: what is my child's refusal to attend school saying to me? The answer might be to spend more time with me, to avoid a teacher they dislike, or to avoid stressful peer relations. As you can see, the answer to this question will help you to arrive at a suitable strategy. But sometimes the answer is not so obvious and often the child might find it difficult to express what it is they are feeling and this can leave parents very confused and stressed. But remember an irrational fear does not always make sense to us. I had a conversation with a student last year who was really struggling with school life. When we explored it further he explained to me that he really was terrified of making a fool of himself in front of a particular group of peers. He told me that he even feared saying his name during roll call for fear he said it incorrectly. This type of social anxiety is becoming more common. Being self-conscious is a normal part of teenage life; however when it is impacting on normal life activity something pathological may be developing. That student told me that he was eating his lunch in the toilet because he didn't want anyone to judge the way he was eating. The sheer isolation that this behaviour was bringing into his life was striking. And it took many conversations to get to the root cause of the issue.

One of the first things I think of when a family comes to me presenting with this problem is, what is this behaviour trying to communicate? All behaviour is a form of communication, so trying to decipher what the behaviour is implicitly telling us is important if there is to be a desirable outcome. I also question what has occurred to cause this maladaptive behaviour and how can it be changed. But as I said at the start of this chapter, sometimes it is not very obvious what is causing the opposition and a child can often struggle to articulate what their concerns are and this can be very challenging for all involved.

The prognosis on school refusal is actually very good. In my experience children generally move away from this behaviour, so it is often about how to support your child when they are going through it so that the behaviour does not become entrenched.

Case Study

The Kearns family came to see me due to their fifteen-year-old son's refusal to go to school. They had become very concerned when the school contacted them over their child's absenteeism. Of course, news that their child had missed over twenty days of school was as shocking as it was surprising to them. In his early conversations the boy outlined how he would get on the bus so his parents would think he was going to school and would literally get the next bus back to where he had come from and spend the day on his own in the house while his parents were at work. The following is a session I had when the whole family was present: Mum (Natasha), Dad (Jim), Nancy (13) and Connor (15).

Richard: Today we are going to hear from everyone in the family and about what it is like to live in the house. I'm going to ask Nancy to talk first because you are the youngest; I was the youngest in my family Nancy – so we have to stick together. I'm going to ask the rest of you to listen to Nancy as if she was not your child or sister and please don't interrupt her. Everyone will get a chance to express their own feelings and sentiments to a particular narrative but it is important that everyone has time to speak their story. So Nancy, what has it been like in the house?

Nancy: Thanks, no one ever asks me first. I like living at home but there is a lot of shouting. Especially after the school rang to tell on Connor.

Richard: Where were you when all of this was going on?

Nancy: I stayed in my room. That's where I normally am. I don't mind though. I just put in my earphones and listen to music.

Richard: So you escape into music?

Nancy: Yeah, sure it's nothing to do with me.

Richard: If I had a magic wand, and I could make everything as you would like it to be, what would be different than it is now?

Nancy: Dunno; less shouting. Connor would stay out of my room. That's it.

Richard: So, it's the shouting that you would like to end?

Nancy: Yeah, and for Mum and Dad to give Connor a break. He tries hard.

Richard: Can you explain what you mean by 'he tries hard'?

Nancy: He tries to do well in school, but they don't see that. They only see all the other stuff.

Richard: What is that?
Nancy: The reason we are here: missing school, anxiety, bad mood, shouting – that stuff.
Richard: Thank you for being so honest. I'm sure that must be hard for you to describe in front of everyone; you are very brave.
Nancy: Thanks for asking me first.
Richard: Connor, can you describe what it is like for you living in the house.
Connor: It's okay. I mean I know Mum and Dad worry about me. But I'm okay.
Richard: Are you okay?
Connor: Not really.
Richard: What made you say you were okay there?
Connor: I don't want to upset my parents.
Richard: Do you think they would be upset if they knew you were not okay?
Connor: Yes. (Connor is beginning to cry at this point.)
Richard: If your tears could talk what would they be saying to me now?
Connor: Sorry for letting you down Dad.
Richard: In what way have you let Dad down?
Connor: I'm not sporty; I'm not academic; I'm not the son he wanted.
Richard: Why do you think Dad wanted a sporty, academic son? Not that you are not those things but why do you feel that?
Connor: I'm not like Dad. He was sporty and academic; I'm not. I hate school.
Richard: What in particular do you dislike about school?
Connor: I dunno; it's just like when I get near to school I feel this sudden sickness, my stomach does somersaults. I panic I guess. I just can't face it.
Richard: Can you describe that panic a bit more?
Connor: It's difficult but I just feel sick. My heart is racing and I want to throw up.

Richard: Okay, thanks for being so honest. I'm going to ask you to do something that may be a little strange. I'm going to talk directly to that panic, if you don't mind.

Connor: Okay.

(I place a black mat on the table and explain that this mat is his panic and I'm going to ask it a series of questions and he has to answer for it in the first person. This is a very useful technique I use to allow a child or teenager to express a feeling they might find difficult to express themselves. This allows for the genuine expression of a complicated emotion in a safe way.)

Richard: Hi, what should I call you?

Connor: Black Mass.

Richard: Okay, thank you Black Mass for allowing me to talk to you.

Connor: You're welcome.

Richard: You are more polite than I thought you would be. Can I ask you a few questions?

Connor: Yes.

Richard: When did Connor first know you were there?

Connor: When he was about ten.

Richard: Can you describe what was going on at the time?

Connor: Connor was at a birthday party and he felt unsure of himself.

Richard: So you popped up then?

Connor: Yes.

Richard: Do you only pop up when he is feeling vulnerable?

Connor: Yes. And when he is feeling anxious.

Richard: What do you say to him?

Connor: Run away, don't feel this. Get away.

Richard: Where did you come from?

Connor: I dunno; I was always there.

Richard: So, you there before he was ten?

Connor: Yes, but Connor didn't know.

Richard: Are you a friend of Connor's or enemy?

Connor: He thinks I'm a friend but I'm an enemy.

Richard: What would need to happen for you to leave Connor?
Connor: Connor would need to feel happy in himself.
Richard: When are you most silent?
Connor: When Connor is having a good time with Dad.
Richard: Can you describe a situation when you are quiet?
Connor: When Dad cooks for Connor and they watch a movie together, then I'm quiet.
Richard: Are you happy then?
Connor: I guess not, but Connor is.
Richard: What would make Connor happy in himself?
Connor: Connor would have to feel confident and that he doesn't let his Dad down.
Richard: So are you there because Connor wants to be like his Dad?
Connor: Yes.
Richard: Are you there during school?
Connor: Yes, I tell him to leave or shout something to get him in trouble or to not do his homework so they know I'm there.
Richard: So you want people to know you are there?
Connor: Yes.
Richard: Okay, thank you Connor for helping with that conversation. That was really interesting, and I couldn't have had that without your help.
Connor: You're welcome.
Richard: Okay Mum and Dad, what was that like to listen to? Who would like to speak first?
Ray: That was hard to listen to; I've never wanted Connor to be like me. I want him to be himself.
Natasha: Ray is a really good father, he loves his children. But he had a difficult relationship with his own father. So, I think that might be present in his relationship with Connor.
Richard: Thanks for that.
Ray: My father was strict. He was a difficult man to please; I never want Connor to please me.

> Connor: But you do; you say things like, 'come on Connor, it's not that hard. When I was young I didn't struggle with this stuff.'
> Richard: What stuff is Dad referring to here?
> Connor: Maths; whatever subject I'm finding difficult.
> Richard: Would you agree with Connor's perception of things?
> Ray: I suppose I do say things like that. But I don't mean them. I suppose I feel Connor is lucky to have a father who is engaged and wants the best for him, I never remember my own father ever taking an interest in my homework or life for that matter.
> Nancy: I think this is the issue.
> Richard: Can you explain what you mean, Nancy?
> Nancy: Ray wants to prove to Connor that he is interested in his life but does it in a way that smothers Connor.
> Ray: Maybe that's true.
> Connor: It is.
> Richard: And when you are getting off the bus Connor what is that feeling saying to you?
> Connor: Run away because if you don't Dad will know you are not like him.

Case Study Explained

Here we can clearly see what is going on within this family unit and the pressure it is placing on Connor. Ray's difficult relationship with his own father is positioning him in a difficult relationship with his son. In his endeavour to support his child he is fracturing his relationship with him. Often, when we have a negative relationship growing up we decide never to replicate that relational dynamic but paradoxically in our efforts to avoid that we bring into life the very thing we are trying to escape from. What I mean by this is what we see here: Ray wants to have a close relationship with Connor but is in fact driving Connor away and without intervention Ray will create the very same relationship with his son as he had with his father. Ray's desire to help Connor – because his father did not help him – leads him to say things like 'I didn't struggle like this when I was your age' or 'my father didn't help me, you don't know how lucky you are.' Connor doesn't feel lucky to have a father who makes him feel stupid. And that certainly isn't Ray's objective. They have become trapped in this relational dynamic and this happens to so many parents and children. Often we launch negative comments when our competencies are being tested. I see this frequently in my work in schools. Teachers sit around the table discussing students they are finding difficult to manage so they say things like 'he's weak', 'he's lazy' – labelling conversations like these ones are very negative for the child's successful outcome in that school environment. And why is the teacher launching such comments? Well unfortunately their competencies are being tested but they are unaware of this or do not want to face this difficult realisation so they firmly place the locus of the problem within the child because 'they are lazy': it's not my issue, it's theirs. And as parents we often do this too. When we find one of our children difficult to manage we can launch the same kind of narratives about our children. But labels do not predict the future, they write them.

So, think of the child who is challenging you – how do you speak about them? I had a parent once who refused to call his child by his name; he referred to him as 'that child' for three sessions until I pointed out that he had not in fact used his name in the sessions. What followed was a very painful conversation about how he felt completely useless as a father and that his son had really exposed some of the insecurities he held as a parent. It was understanding this that helped father and son in their relationship. In Ray and Connor's case it was helping Ray see how his relationship with his own father was present in his relationship with his son that really brought about change in how they communicated with each other. It took that externalising conversation, where they were introduced to the 'black mass' that Connor was labouring with, to bring about a significant change in how Connor viewed his father and himself.

In my work with adolescents a commonality among those who are able to manage their anxiety is a healthy sense of self, or what we call self-esteem. A child can have a negative sense of self for myriad reasons. But the good news is that you can help your child to develop a new, more positive understanding of themselves.

How to Build Your Child's Self-Esteem
What Is Self-Esteem?

Self-esteem is one of those rare, intangible and unquantifiable aspects of the human condition. It is nearly easier not to see than to see. And, as parents, it can often leave us mystified as how to promote and nurture it within our children. As a schoolteacher working with adolescents over the last fifteen years, talking about self-esteem is one of the most frequent recurring conversations I have with parents about their child. Yet I have often found myself struggling for the correct language to express what exactly it is I am trying to say. Low self-esteem or poor view of self can have a devastating impact on a child that can last a lifetime, and lead them into a series of destructive relationships. The famous family therapist Murray Bowen believed that children who cannot separate their own intellectual and emotional functioning from the family develop what he called 'low differentiation of self'. What he meant by this is that children who present with 'low differentiation of self' constantly seek the approval and acceptance of others and often either conform themselves to please others or attempt to force others to conform to them. He suggested that those presenting with 'low differentiation of self' often seek out people who have a similar poor view of self and therefore enter into relationships in adulthood that are destructive and doomed before they begin. So, developing your child's view of self and their place in the world which allows them to have independent thoughts from the family system is one of the most significant and challenging endeavours a parent can be engaged in. A healthy self-esteem is when a child values themselves. When they believe they have the tools to manage their daily life and don't become too fazed by change. A child who has a positive sense of self is not easily lead, and doesn't follow the crowd without question.

Five Tips to Build Your Child's Self-Esteem

1. Reward failure as well as success. Children can often become caught in the pursuit of perfection in order to please a parent. It is very satisfying for a child when they are rewarded for winning or succeeding at something. However, what happens when they are not successful? Children must learn that losing or not being the best is an important part of life. If the message is given to children that failure is not acceptable they will never fully enjoy the pursuit they are engaged in.
2. Treat each child individually. When parents tell their children that they love them the same, this can cause competition between siblings as they vie for their parent's love and attention. What I often tell my daughters is that I love them the same amount but differently. This removes the competitive nature of my love and allows the children to enjoy the uniqueness of each relationship.
3. Allow your child to have a say in family matters. When we exclude our children from decision-making we are implicitly telling them that their opinion does not matter. We all want to create children who value themselves and believe that they have something valuable to offer the world. Childhood is the time to reinforce that their opinion does count and it is valued. Something as arbitrary as allowing your child to decide what you do on a Sunday can significantly impact on a child's sense of self-worth.
4. Praise the uniqueness of your child's strengths. There is something inherently Irish about the way we seem to be more focused on what we can't do than what we can do. Children, in particular, gauge themselves by comparing their skills to their peers. As parents, we need to shift that negative focus and help them to see the positive aspects of themselves.
5. Be by your child's side, not on it. There is a lot in this simple phrase that can impact positively on your child self-esteem. We must allow our children to fail as well as to succeed. When we become overly identified with our child's perceived slights or

failings we can often model co-dependency or create Bowen's 'low differentiation of self'.

Developing your child's self-esteem is a life-long task, and something that challenges all of us as parents. But if we encourage our children and listen to them in a supportive way we can help them to develop coping strategies for when those challenges arrive in their life. Often we confuse helping our child with making our child helpless. I had a couple come to me recently because their 24-year-old son had dropped out of college for the third year in a row. The mother asked a very important question early on in the sessions: 'how did we get here?' This is a question I hear a lot in my practice. And the answer generally follows shortly after, as it did in this case. Her husband described how his wife had done everything for their son: wash and iron his clothes, make his dinners, even make him hot milk before bed. She had even started ringing his friends to organise his weekends for him. As her husband described the situation in the house, I could see her become visibly agitated. It wasn't long before she uttered the following words: 'so it's all my fault, is it?' But it really isn't about blame; it's about understanding how our behaviours, as parents, impact on how our children learn to navigate the world. That case was very interesting, because the mother admitted to her fear of losing her son. She had a very poor relationship with her other sons and was terrified that she was going to lose her youngest son also. And in her bid to keep him she had made him low functioning. It wasn't until she acknowledged what her behaviour was doing to her child that there was any real significant shift in her son's life.

> "If I defer the grief, I will diminish the gift." – Evan Boland

I have noticed over the years, working in schools, that children are finding it more and more difficult to cope with adversity. And I have often wondered what is happening in the home that is preventing children from developing coping mechanisms when they encounter a challenge. We all want our children to be happy, but we know life will throw them a curve ball at times – so our children need to be able to deal with that curve ball when it comes hurtling towards them. I had a conversation with a parent recently about whether or not she should take her child out of school because he was finding it difficult to settle in. Of course, it can be very traumatic to watch your child suffer. And our first reaction can be to fix the problem immediately so our child will not suffer but we are only delaying the grief for a later date. If children do not develop the ability to handle difficult situations, which will inevitably arrive, they will find adulthood incredibly problematic. We must, as parents, help to build their resilience. That parent, after our conversation, did not remove her child but in fact sent him on a school trip with his peers. He forged new relationships not only with his peers but also with himself. His parents gave him a very important gift: they had taught him resilience. If they had changed schools, what lesson would have been learned? That when things get difficult there is always a get-out-of-jail card? This does not happen in the adult world. We must not diminish our children by telling them we think they do not have the strength to deal with adversity. Our children are far more resilient than we give them credit for.

Recently my own daughter was sitting at the table doing her homework while I was in the kitchen preparing the dinner. I could hear her beginning to moan about all the work she had to do. It wasn't long before she was standing in front of me, tears in her puppy eyes staring up, pleading with me:

Hannah: Will you write a note to my teacher please?
Richard: Why?
Hannah: It's not fair; I have so much homework to do and you don't.
Richard: What would the note say?
Hannah: That I couldn't do my homework because I was tired.
Richard: What would you be doing if not your homework?
Hannah: Playing Barbies with my sister.
Richard: Well, we all have to do things we don't like; I have to correct these college essays later, and I don't want to do that but I have to. And the longer you stay here with me giving out

about it the less time you will have to play Barbies with your sister.

I then took out the essays and started to correct them in front of her. At this my daughter went back into the room and started doing her homework. Now, think about the message my daughter would have received if I had written her a note and excused her from her homework that night. She would have learned that when things got difficult or when a challenge arose I would step in and fix it for her. And that is not a helpful message for your child to learn. In my experience I think this is what is happening at the moment. Parents are confusing this drive for well-being to mean their child most never experience adversity rather than helping their child to develop the skills to overcome adversity when it arises. These parents, even though they are well-intentioned, are doing their children such a disservice by removing them from every potential learning moment in their life.

How to Build Your Child's Resilience

- *Teach your child how to reframe.* This is a psychological tool we use to help our clients to see things differently and it is very useful for children. I remember being on the sideline of a rugby match chatting to a parent who was eagerly waiting for his child to play. At the end of the game his son came over, clearly disappointed, and said 'I only played for ten minutes'. His father hugged him and said 'yeah, but it was some ten minutes.' That was a wonderful reframe.
- *Model resilience.* Show your child a situation where you didn't succeed but you dealt with that failure in a positive way. Teach them that failure is a part of success. Sir James Dyson said in an interview once, 'we have to embrace failure; you don't have to bother being creative if the first time you do something, it works.' I find TED talks are a great resource for adolescents on a variety of themes, and there are plenty on building resilience. Show them to your teenager. It really inspires them when

they hear someone they admire talk about how they dealt with failure.
- *Don't join them in their upset.* When your child comes to you with an issue do not try to solve it for them. Instead, ask them questions about the issue and what it means for them. Allow them to figure it out. Be supportive without disempowering them.

Resilience is not something that some children are born with and some are not. We teach our children how to cope with situations through our actions and our words. If the message is relayed to a child that they are not able to deal with adversity they will struggle as they make their way through life. We all know that our children are going to face difficulties – our job, as parents, is to teach them how to handle those difficulties when they arise.

9

Perfectionism, Body Image and Steroid Use

I'm including a chapter on steroid use in this book because I have been struck over the years with the number of parents coming to me looking for help with their child's obsession with appearance. There is no doubt about it: social media, with its reliance on image platforms such as Instagram, has driven this interest in aesthetics. I think this an important chapter for any parent of a teenager in today's world because your child doesn't have to be involved in competitive sports to be engaged in such a dangerous activity as ingesting anabolic steroids. In fact, the figures show that a new demographic of steroid users has emerged over the last number of years. This new demographic has come to light with the surge in teenagers seeking out services like needle exchange.

Perfectionism, Body Image and Steroid Use

This new clientele are looking for clean needles so that they can take a course of steroids to get their body in shape for their summer holiday with their friends. This is one of the most shocking new developments in steroid use in this country and illuminates the need for parents to be aware of what is going on in their child's peer group. Whom you child associates with and hangs out with is a very good indicator of their interests and what sort of behaviours they will get involved in.

Traditionally this pressure on appearance was something girls laboured with – having to look a certain way or wear certain clothes to fit in with the demands of their peer group. This is still very much the case, and perhaps has even worsened with the growth of social media. However, in recent years boys have also come under increasing pressure to achieve some sort of notion of what a young body should look like. So it is very important that you monitor your child's emerging interest in body image. Early intervention is always far more desirable; we have to open up a dialogue with our children around the issue of appearance because they are subjected to a barrage of images at any given moment during their day that promotes a certain body type as ideal. And we must talk to them about the reality of appearance and help them to develop a healthy self-esteem so that their confidence is not caught up in their body image.

One of the most overt shifts in the teenage world I have noticed working with teenagers in schools over the last eighteen years is the sheer level of determination and commitment to self-improvement. When I was growing up as a teenager in the 1990s I never heard of abs or obliques. I never had a conversation about macros and micros. Intermittent fasting was what we did between meals; it certainly wasn't by design. We played sports, but we didn't think about how to build muscle mass or the perfect body fat percentage. It really is only a narrative that has crept into the classroom over the last ten years. With the proliferation of technology, teenagers are swamped with information about how to achieve their desired body shape. Obviously self-improvement is far more desirable than self-destruction, but often teenagers are out there shopping online for products that are harmful and, in some cases, life-threatening. Often in their pursuit of self-improvement teenagers engage in very dangerous behaviours that can have devastating consequences. So, like everything else, parents need to be vigilant and keep an eye on what their child is using to help them get fit. And with tragic stories like the teenager who died in 2018 due to ingesting Stanozolol, a steroid used to build muscle, parents should know how vulnerable and naïve some of our children are when it comes to taking performance-enhancing drugs.

Parents often find that they really do not know how to monitor their child's interest in fitness and sport. What is a healthy interest in keeping fit? And what is an unhealthy interest? When does it become an obsession? And would you notice that your child is over-training and damaging their health? These are very difficult questions to answer. Because, as the literature tells us, to achieve success in any field you have to obsessively train and become consumed with the sport or activity in question. Was David Beckham's obsessive practising of free kicks healthy or unhealthy? Were Rory Gallagher's fingers bleeding while he practised playing guitar as a child an indicator of obsession? Was Tiger Woods' focus as a child normal? Was Steffi Graf's relentless training schedule as a nine-year-old detrimental to her mental health? The list could go on and on, but as we can see these are not easy questions to answer and they would divide any clinical and sports psychologist. However, the one fact we can all agree on is that taking steroids to improve your performance can have deadly consequences and parents must, if they have concerns that their child is taking them, immediately seek professional advice.

SIGNS OF STEROID USE

- *Sudden increase in acne.* It might be difficult to spot this because teenagers often have breakouts in acne due to normal hormonal changes during adolescence. But, if you are concerned about your child's obsessive exercising and increased size it might be an early indicator of steroid use.
- *Increased aggression or irritableness.* This behavioural change is a significant factor to monitor. If your child has suddenly become aggressive or irritable about the slightest thing again it

could be a red flag that something is not right and it could be a sign of steroid use.
- *Change in social group.* When a child suddenly switches social groups it is generally a warning sign that something significant has taken place. It could mean the group they have left did not approve of what they were doing, so they may have sought out a group that will not be judgemental or even condone a risky behaviour. Of course, there may be innocent reasons for changing friends but if you are concerned about those earlier signs, coupled with peer group change, I would contact your child's former friends and/or their parents and question them as to why your child has left that particular group of friends. You would be surprised what a peer group knows and is willing to tell you if approached in a sensitive way.
- *Obsessive talking about building muscle.* As I said, what is obsessive and unhealthy is very difficult to diagnose for parents, but if you notice that the only conversation from your teenager is pertaining to fitness and building muscle it could be a sign that they are becoming obsessed with building the perfect body and often this leads teenagers to take shortcuts to achieve quick results.

Steroid use is no longer confined to the murky underworld of some professional top athletes. The internet has quite literally brought them into your child's bedroom. If you are concerned about your child's sudden and rapid increase in muscle size and you have noticed some of the signs outlined above, consult your local doctor and explain your fears. You should also check your child's bedroom for steroid paraphernalia. Often children are careless with packaging, as they believe you will not know what to look for. Become familiar with steroids and what they look like and the packaging they come in. If you find a suspicious wrapper, bring it to your local doctor and seek advice as to your next step. Hopefully your child's interest in sports is a healthy one but if you are concerned about some of the issues I have discussed seek advice: you are not alone and your child may need your help.

PERFECTIONISM

An aspect of modern life that feeds this desire for a particular body image is the concept of perfectionism. I have been struck over the years talking with teenagers how much pressure they put on themselves to achieve the perfect body, exam, relationship, picture – the list could go on. Nothing will bring about a sense of failure more rapidly than the desperate, futile pursuit of perfection. Because there is no perfect. But TV shows like *Love Island*, where cosmetically enhanced girls and overly buffed boys vie for each other's attention, illuminates the interest in this type of body image because it is the most-watched show in recent times. Nothing captures what I'm saying here more than the 'selfie'. Cameras are now pointing inwards rather than outwards; we are in the age of extreme individualism. Being yourself and being an individual are positive pursuits; however not when it becomes pathological. And we have to mind our children as they navigate this new phenomenon, because it can lead to very serious conditions like eating disorders. I have had far too many conversations in my clinic with young teenage girls who described the same starting point: the desire to control how they were perceived by their peers and their image on social media. An eating disorder is a very complicated and difficult condition to treat and it can bring so much upheaval for the family trying to support their child struggling with it. So helping your child to manage this new obsession with perfection and body image is an important first step in combating it if your child's issue is rooted in body image. As I said, it is a complicated disorder to work with and often it is about control and power more than body image.

Of course social media platforms like Instagram and Snapchat are a major reason why there has been such a sudden rise in this modern phenomenon but they are only part of the story. We have to ask ourselves, where are they receiving the messages that a particular body type is desirable? Social media, with its reliance on images, is certainly a cause, but maybe it's an easy target; I think there are wider issues here. If we actually stop and look around us and view the messages our children are receiving we can clearly see why they hold the belief they must look a certain way. Pictures on Instagram generally use a filter, and billboards with emaciated models are ubiquitous and give teenagers all the wrong messages. The reason why I am writing about this is because I hear it so often in my clinic – teenage boys and girls describing their absolute hatred of their own body. It is something I find myself becoming increasingly frustrated and angry with: hearing these beautiful young children, with their whole lives ahead of them, speaking about themselves in such hostile and negative ways just because they don't have a six-pack or a certain body fat index. We must, as policymakers, teachers and parents, work to prevent our children from receiving such damaging messages about body image. We must also work with them to help them understand that certain body types are not healthy and often take extremely undesirable methods to achieve and some are not even real – they have been photoshopped. And our children are falling prey to such images. We need to start educating them about body image and self-esteem. Our job, as parents, is to help our children correctly interpret the messages they are receiving. This is vitally important when it comes to body image because, as I have said, those messages are everywhere.

Body image develops during the formative years and is influenced by family and culture. That is why parents must work vigilantly with their children to debunk the ubiquitous bombardment of false body images they receive in the media. Everywhere you look we are surrounded by hyper-fit, buff young males and painfully thin young women with artificially enhanced breasts. There has been a huge increase in the amount of young adults seeking out cosmetic surgery in this country. Why is that? Because we are falling for the messages we are receiving. As parents, we must explain the nature of advertising versus reality. We have far too many tragic examples of the consequences of what happens when our children cannot see past their desire for that perfect body image to turn a blind eye. A new trend is teenagers transiently using steroids before they head off on a summer holiday to get in shape. Their lack of knowledge about and experience with these heavy anabolic steroids is one of the main reasons why we have a litany of so many terrible and tragic stories in our society.

Often big muscles are associated with a strong, healthy body. But the irony can be that the methods used to attain such a big physique can be anything but healthy. An obsession with body image can destroy a teenager's self-esteem. It is vitally important that we help our children navigate the plethora of messages they are receiving. I find myself talking more and more to teenagers about this issue in the classroom. I try to explain to them about the nature of social construction and how body image is simply a construct and like everything we construct it will go in and out of fashion. As I show them different body types that were in fashion at one point and are no longer, I can see the pressure lifting off them as they become aware of the spell they have been under. I leave them with this question: do you want to be a slave to the advertisers who are simply after your money? There is nothing more beautiful than the uniqueness of you, celebrate that – never conform to someone else's idea of what you should be. This kind of conversation lifts the fog of advertising. Teenagers really don't like the idea that they are simply following a trend or that they are victims of advertising so that big companies can make money, so when they are introduced to this fact it can really change how they view body image.

10

Sleep Deprivation and Exams

There are so many challenging relationships we have to navigate in our daily lives: our peer group, colleagues and family all demand incredible political acumen to traverse without conflict. But there are other relationships, ones that are more innocuous, subtler and yet drive us crazy at times. And while our relationship with family and friends are, to some extent, within our control, some relationships seem like they are not. One of the most complex and problematic relationships I have in my life is my relationship with sleep. She has been a cruel mistress over the years. The night before my Leaving Certificate she was nowhere to be seen; I vividly remember begging, praying even, for her to arrive, but she did not obey my desperate pleas. I yawned my way through that first exam. In fact, over the years, the more I looked for her the more diaphanous that chief nourisher in life's feast became.

And yet, the night before my wedding I slept like the proverbial log. As I said, it's complicated.

The loss of sleep is a common aliment; us sapiens have always had an unusual relationship with it. A deep sleep has not always been a good thing for our survival. So, we are suspicious of it, and yet we need it to survive. They say if you live for ninety years you will spend a third of that time – thirty-two years to be exact – supine and still. But for many of us that quiet time can really be challenging. Sleep deprivation occurs when an individual gets less sleep than they need to feel awake and alert. The amount of sleep an individual needs varies from person to person but on average teenagers need 8–10 hours to be alert the following day, while adults need slightly less, averaging about 7–8 hours. Why do we sleep? Well, scientists and sleep specialists all agree we sleep to rejuvenate the body. However, for most of us, we are functioning on minimal sleep. And in my experience teenagers are the biggest sufferers of sleep deprivation and they are the very ones who need it the most.

Sleep impacts teenagers when they are suffering stressful events in their life. One of the biggest stressors for a teenager is the state exam. These are three facts about sleep deprivation you should know to support your teenager through exams:

1. Loss of sleep alters normal functioning of attention, and disrupts the ability to focus on environmental sensory input. When you think about this fact it is easy to understand why so many students, in the lead-up to exams, struggle with getting enough sleep. Stress impacts our ability to sleep, so when students become stressed they lose sleep and this in turn impacts the ability to function highly the next day, which prevents them from being able to reach the levels of concentration required for learning off subject material and this causes more stress. So, it becomes a desperate negative cycle for the student. I have many conversations with students concerning this cycle.
2. Not getting enough sleep prevents the body from strengthening the immune system. That is why teenagers often get sick during the weeks leading up to the exams. They are rundown

and susceptible to infection, because lack of sleep depletes the body's ability to reproduce cytokines, which fight off infection.
3. Insufficient sleep impacts on a teenager's metabolism. The less sleep they have the more insulin they produce, which increases fat storage so when they eat foods like carbohydrates for energy their body will more rapidly store it as fat.

Schools are becoming far more aware of the importance of sleep: I often get invited to schools to talk to students and parents about how to develop healthy sleep patterns. Education seems to be changing to support students to cope with the demands placed on them by the points system. This is a very positive thing, because the pressure on them is immense. In 2018 a student in the Institute of Education was one of six students in the country to achieve 6 H1s. I mention her because she is a remarkable and inspiring young lady. She obviously studied well but she also was very balanced in her approach: she kept up her extracurricular activities like tennis and still managed to have a social life. One of the key aspects of her success, she told me, was finishing study before 10 p.m. in the evening so that she could unwind before going to sleep. She acknowledged that a restful sleep was so important to her success. Students need to hear a narrative like that, because they often mistakenly think they have to give up everything to do well in their exams: friends, sport and even sleep. And their mental health suffers as a result. Achieving your goal in the Leaving Certificate is not only about studying hard but also about having a healthy approach to that study. And getting the required sleep so that your brain is nourished is a vital component in that success. Sleep is a crucial part of a healthy day ahead and yet, at times, we can have such a difficult relationship with it.

Remember, children need boundaries and parents are the ones who must help their child to navigate the world. A healthy relationship with sleep is developed in those formative years. Often we can get caught thinking that sleep is something we can't control. I regularly hear parents launch the same ill-fated label: 'He's just a bad sleeper, that's all.' If we believe this, well then, there is nothing we can do. He is powerless to sleep deprivation and he must learn to live with the consequences of exhaustion. However, if we look at sleep in a systemic way and examine what his sleeping habits are and ask a few basic questions – like what is preoccupying his mind before he sleeps? What is he ruminating on that disturbs a peaceful state of mind and why? How does he unwind and what makes him restful? – we might actually start a therapeutic conversation about sleep that has the ability to change his sleeping patterns for the better.

FIVE STEPS TO A BETTER NIGHT'S SLEEP

1. Increase bright light exposure during the day. It is often very difficult in Ireland to get enough bright light during the winter months. But research shows that exposure to bright light helps to keep your internal clock, known as the circadian rhythm, in check. Natural sunlight or bright light keeps this healthy. You might find investing in a bright light device one of the first major steps to overcoming sleep deprivation.
2. Reduce blue light exposure. Nothing has invaded our personal worlds quite like technology. More and more students are coming to me with sleep deprivation and when I look at their habits technology and blue light is certainly one of the main reasons why they are struggling to get sufficient rest. Smartphones and laptops emit a light known as blue light and this impacts melatonin production, which regulates sleep. Downloading an app like f.lux will help reduce the glare of blue light on your devices. Avoid using smartphones and other electronic devices in the two hours before bedtime, and while in bed.
3. Get consistent with your sleep times. Often what can happen is we have a restless night's sleep so we over-sleep the following day, or worse we nap during the day. This is not a desirable habit to get into because it is not consistent and you are not training your body when it should be sleeping. Inconsistent sleeping patterns will only serve to disrupt sleep. If you have a bad night's sleep you should get up at your normal time and work your normal day, avoid naps and go to sleep the following night at the time you normally go to sleep, therefore

creating a consistent pattern. You will be thankful for this in the long run.
4. Make your sleeping environment appealing. Often bedrooms are very untidy, cluttered places with clothes and books everywhere. A bedroom should be slightly cold, tidy and have clean bedsheets for optimal chance of sleep. Remember it's far more difficult for your mind to turn off if it is surrounded by chaos. So change your bedroom environment. Make it a place of tranquillity. I had a client once tell me that his wife called his wardrobe 'the bad mood press'. He said she called it this because every time she opened it, it put her in a bad mood because clothes would fall out. An environment like that is not conducive for sleep.
5. What makes you relax? Personally I find reading before I sleep very relaxing and it tires my mind. Maybe you don't like reading, maybe you prefer yoga or listening to music; whatever it is, figuring out what relaxes you and tires your mind will be an important step to achieving a peaceful night's sleep. Also relax about sleep, if you don't get a good night's sleep, don't panic – you'll get it the next night. Often people put themselves under pressure to sleep, which has the opposite outcome.

A good night's sleep is so important for the day ahead. Teenagers need to be supported in their relationship with sleep. As parents, we must have a policy in the house that removes technology from the bedroom. When we notice our children are not rested and are in fact exhausted we must ask ourselves what has happened to their sleeping pattern and how can I support them to get that pattern back on track. Doing well in exams and indeed in life is not about pulling 'all-nighters' and being excessive in your approach to the work you have to do but rather it is about being measured and consistent, and enjoying the downtime in each day.

11

The Modern Family

There have been significant changes in what is meant by the family and family life over the last number of years in this country. Theorists put forward the idea that family life and what goes on behind closed doors can be viewed as a microcosm for what is occurring in society as a whole, or conversely it is argued that the ills of society often manifest in the family. The health of our family system is a clear indicator of the health of our society. Interestingly enough, Ireland has the lowest divorce rate in Europe, with only 0.7 in every 1,000 people divorcing. There are obviously many complicated factors feeding into that statistic: ideologies and discourses inherent in our society and how family law goes about its business all impact on our ideas about the family and what family life should be like. Whichever way you look at it, the traditional nuclear family has dramatically changed over the

The Modern Family

last number of years. The number of same-sex marriages will continue to increase while many couples decide not to get married and there are increasing variations on what shape a family takes, such as single-parent families and blended families. The age profile of those getting married has shifted too. In the mid-1960s the average couple getting married were in their mid-twenties; in modern times couples are now marrying in their mid- to late thirties. So, couples are getting married later in life and generally having children at a later age. Also, there is greater diversity in people's expectations, such that men are no longer expected to be the sole earners and expectations have certainly expanded about greater sharing of domestic roles, such as childcare and house work.

While many of these changes have had a positive impact on the family, others have damaged or ruptured the ecology of the family. And the rupture I'm speaking to here does not find too much expression in our society but it's there; its muted presence often finds a voice in my clinic. I regularly meet women in the therapeutic setting who are overwhelmed because of the amount of work placed on them to keep the family going both financially and emotionally. It seems, in some cases, that these expanding expectations often place huge pressure on women because even if they have a full-time job they still tend to take on the bulk of domestic duties, not to mention frequently caring for their elderly parents. You could ask who am I to talk about a woman's role in the house, but I see it and hear it so loudly in my work: women are placing incredible strain on themselves to be everything to everyone within the family unit. It is not sustainable for a healthy family system. The reason I'm speaking about it here is so that mothers look at the amount of work they take on in their daily lives. Because they so often take on too much. The burden to be all things to all people that women labour with can damage their mental health. I see it in my clinic too much not to speak about it. Women exhausted and emotionally drained because of the demands they have allowed to be placed on them. We get assigned roles so quickly in families. 'The good daughter', 'the responsible one': these labels are designed to keep us in a particular position within the family. And often they are not healthy roles for a woman to be in. Often those roles are filled with the burden of duty. When I talk to a woman who is overwhelmed by the responsibility in her life I regularly hear the same voice, the desire to be 'the good child'. It is often debunking that notion and analysing where it took root in her childhood that helps to free her from the chains of her childhood.

Much of the therapeutic work I do is helping parents to build boundaries in the family dynamic so that they can confidently tell their children 'no' when they are confronted by unreasonable demands. It is important that children hear 'no' because it prevents them from developing unrealistic expectations about the world. And yet we can, as parents, be quite slow to say that magic word, even when we know we should. In my experience I have yet to meet an adult who said, 'I must really thank my parents for giving into my every whim.' I have certainly met adults who said, 'my parents always gave into my demands – I never had to face consequences, maybe that's why I struggle to compromise.' This type of mentality is destructive for a young developing mind. We all need to hear a firm 'no' at times. So, saying 'no' is an important part of parenting, but another facet of life where we need to become more comfortable with saying 'no' is in our own personal life. Many of the clients I work with have sought out therapy because the balance in their life is off. They know the reason for this imbalance but feel at a loss as to what to do. They have become overwhelmed with the amount of work or responsibilities they have taken on and do not know how to pull back to protect their mental health from collapsing.

Why is it we take on too much? And what can we do to prevent burnout or becoming overwhelmed with our daily lives? This is something most of us have to work on, because becoming overwhelmed can so easily creep up on us if we are not vigilant about the workload we allow to be placed on us. Being effective in the family is not about the amount of work you do but how you manage your time and how you manage the time you are away from the family. If you allow all of your time to be consumed with family and work you will quickly burn out. You improve your efficacy when you are fresh and excited for the day ahead. Bill Gates recently said that it wasn't until he saw Warren Buffett's weekly schedule that he realised he was not utilising his time correctly. Gates explained that being busy is not 'a proxy of your seriousness' and that time management is an integral component of being successful. Time is the one thing we cannot buy. And if you pack your time with an unrealistic workload or responsibilities you will collapse.

As I said, I see this with many of the women who come into my clinic. The pressure they have placed on themselves because they find it so hard to say 'no' to whatever has been asked of them. I often feel the pressure in the room as they delineate their daily routine: drop the kids to school, go to work, collect the kids, drop them at various activities, make the dinner, visit their parents, collect the kids, wash the uniforms and prepare for the next day. It is generally an exhaustive litany of banal routine that would cause the burnout of the most stoic and resilient among us. When I ask the simple question, 'where are you in all of this?' they immediately understand what I am saying and acknowledge that they have to change something because they are becoming lost in routine. As parents we are busy. There is no getting away from that. Dropping and collecting kids and making dinners and all the rest of what goes with being a parent can consume our daily lives. But we must work to find balance or things will fall apart. The centre will not hold if you are constantly in a state of frenzied movement. So, what can that mother do to better manage the responsibilities she has? This is such an important question.

Firstly, it should not all land on her lap. As parents you must sit down and make a sensible plan of who is going to do what during the week. Dividing up responsibilities ensures one parent isn't taking on too much. Also, our children cannot do every activity or go on every play date. So, do not feel guilty for saying 'no' to something that places incredible strain on your day. We can often get caught running around from play date to play date like headless chickens. Your child does not need to go on so many play dates. By pulling back a little and dividing up the chores during the week, that little space you find could make all the difference.

It is so important that you find time to check in with yourself. Just because you're a parent doesn't mean you lose yourself in the process. Often we have to work at staying connected to ourselves – that is not a selfish act but rather a vital one if we are to remain happy and healthy in our role as parent. Remember, a healthy family system is one that allows for you to be a part of and separate from it.

Men's roles are shifting too. If a man wants to stay at home and rear his children does he become a source of derision? In most cases I would say he does. What does that say about us and how far we've progressed? With children spending increasing hours in childcare and after-school services, it is easy to assume that the family is in crisis, and this can also be viewed as a fundamental threat to the stability of society. Because, as I said, society and the family are linked. Of course men need to step up here too and look at the amount of pressure on their partner in the house. Men have had a very clear role over the years and now that is shifting and the expectations on them as to what they should be like as a partner and father has evolved dramatically; they must also make sure that the bulk of responsibility is not one-sided. And men are less secure or certain in their role too. This is a very challenging time for the family so there needs to be a clear conversation about how you want your family to run. All systems fall into their own unique patterns but that does not mean they cannot change. The family is by far the most complicated system we have, and it has become far more complicated over the last number of years with how our society has progressed. We must make sure in all that complexity there is room for tradition and simplicity too. We must make sure that everyone in that system understands how it works and their role within it. Nothing impacts the type of person we become more than the family we grow up in. It is vital that, as we move into setting up our own family, we let the labels from our childhood go and avoid carrying forward any negative patterns of communication we may have experienced in our family of origin.

Managing the Wider Family

When we move into our middle life we have so many relationships to navigate. Some of the most complicated relationships we will ever have to manage in our brief time on this planet are the ones we have with our extended family. And it isn't always easy to hide your true feelings about a certain member of your family unit. So, you have to give yourself a break here too, and realise that you are not always going to get along with everyone and not everyone in that family ecology deserves your friendship. As we get older we generally tend to care less about being liked by everyone, for we come to understand what a futile and exhausting road that can be. However, when clients come to me looking for help with managing difficult relationships I often ask them a series of questions:

- What is it about that person in particular that annoys you?
- What do they bring up for you?
- Whom do they remind you of?
- How are you in that relationship?
- What do you think you contribute to the way you communicate to each other?

Often these questions lead us down the sinuous road of childhood and often I confront a particular type of person they had a negative interaction with and, in some cases, the person they do not like in fact reminds them of themselves. That can be a startling revelation to have and can help to heal that relationship. I believe when we know the context to someone's behaviour it is very difficult to view a person in linear terms and it is also very difficult to judge someone or dislike them, because you now understand their position and why they acted a certain way. So, think about the person you are locked in a difficult relationship with and never look forward to meeting and ask yourself those questions, and answer them honestly. As much as we would like to place the entire blame on someone else, we have to think about how we position that person in any interaction with us.

Often we can hold a particular belief about someone and that belief colours every interaction we have with them. For example, you might think that someone you know is false and gossips a lot, so whenever you are in a conversation with them you tell them nothing about yourself in case you become a source of their gossip, and so they might come to think that you're a distant and cold person, and the negative relational pattern will go on and on until you analyse why you believe that about the person. Maybe they were a gossip but maybe they've changed. Or maybe, just maybe, they act like that around you because they feel that you hold that view of them; labels don't predict the future, they write them. It is challenging the genesis of the presuppositions we hold about people that can really help fix the most complicated of relationships.

And this works for the relationships we have with our children too. Think about the child you are locked in a difficult relationship with. Is there something in the way you are interacting with them that helps to maintain the negative interactions? This is not about blame but trying to understand how we are in the relationship. It is very easy to think of the issue being located within someone else. Try to change that viewpoint and see the wider context of the relationship. This might give you a new way to approach the relationship.

The reason I'm ending this book with a chapter on the family is because the family is the most important and difficult system you will have to manage as you go through life. It never ends and is constantly reshaping. When you marry, you not only take on a partner for life but you also take into your life everyone who orbits your partner's world; to a certain extent when you say 'I do' you are also saying these words to everyone else in your partner's life. And you may need a master's in international diplomacy to get through those relational dynamics unscathed because they are so complicated and laden with landmines that even the most skilled amongst us are found a drift navigating them. Think of Prince Hamlet: 'there is nothing either good nor bad but thinking makes it so'; the next time as you walk into a room filled with both loved and loathed ones, think about how you position people in your relationship with them. We often interact negatively with people because they subconsciously remind us of someone. I have heard the same sentiment uttered so many times in my own clinic: 'I'm hard on them because they remind me of myself.' Often parents are harder on the child who reminds them of themselves because they mistakenly feel they know exactly what that child needs. And in their desperate bid to help the child (which in turn would be helping their younger self) they over-parent them and drive a wedge between themselves and the child who most resembles them. It can be a very healing conversation to have, illuminating this aspect of their relationship. Because none of us want to have a negative relationship with our children, and it can often leave us exasperated and confused as to why one of our children does not respond to us like we would hope. But maybe, just maybe, how we are in that relationship positions our children in their relationship with us. If you notice you are harder on one child because they remind you of yourself, just remember how you felt at that age. Maybe the true gift you could give that child is to pull back and let them figure things out for themselves, like you did.

12

Conclusion

This book has explored the new world of the modern teenager. It has attempted to give some practical advice on how to develop communication with the teenager in your house. It can often feel like you are getting nowhere with your teenager. You put so much into them and all you get back is a grunt. It certainly is challenging. Parents often describe a real sense of loss for the child they once had such a loving and close relationship with. The teenage years can really test the best of us. You have to give yourself a break here too. You're only human and relationships change and shift over the course of life; you cannot stop that from happening. The more you fight against it the more conflict you will have in your house. That doesn't mean you let your child dictate the nature of your relationship with them but you must acknowledge the teenage years are about your child finding their agency and voice. And that isn't always a smooth transition. Your children will push the boundaries. Your child will diminish you at times but how you respond to these conflicts will teach your child how to deal with conflict in their later life.

Often parents say to me, 'his default position is shouting; he screams and roars when he doesn't get what he wants.' When I explore where their child received the message that the appropriate response to a negative stimulus is to shout and roar, in most cases the parents put their hands up and say 'well, that's how my Mum and Dad acted when we were growing up.' We often do not realise how much our children are observing us as templates for human behaviour. When our natural inclination is to shout because we are stressed or worried, we are writing the script of our children's future. And their children will not thank you for passing on this negative behaviour. Of course, we are not robots and we will at times lose our tempers and become anxious. Gaining an insight into what we took from living in our parents' relationship will be very helpful if you really want to see why you hold onto a certain type of behaviour you know is negative and destructive for your child's well-being.

When we set off on this journey with our partners, we both bring a rich and complicated tapestry of stories and held beliefs with us. Understanding each other's context and how it impacts both of you as parents is incredibly significant if you want to change how you are parenting. Often parents, especially those from my generation (born in the late 1960s/1970s), find themselves trying to right the bad parenting techniques used on them with their own children but what actually ends up happening is that they produce the exact same outcome, just in a different way. What I mean by this is that in a parent's bid to hear their child or satiate their child's feelings, they often create a situation whereby the child is never heard or happy. It's one of those strange paradoxes of parenting and something you should look out for. Ask yourself, how was I reared? Does this inform how I parent? What am I trying to avoid in my parenting? Am I falling into the trap? And the trap I'm speaking to here is what happens to many parents. Let's just say your parents were ineffectual and never showed you love. Now you have your own child and you subconsciously or consciously say, 'my child will know they're loved, I will tell them I love them all the time.' What happens here? The child often comes to view the parent's protestations of love as valueless because in their desperate attempt to let their child know they are loved they have diminished the meaning of the word for the child, so the child might come to think they aren't loved because the word has no value. This is just one of the paradoxes that can arise for us as parents. And it is important to think about the type of parent you want to become and what is motivating that desire.

Parenting is not about always getting it right. It's about understanding your child or children and knowing what works for them and what doesn't work. Parenting is by far the most challenging journey we go on as adults. When we say 'I do' or set out on a relationship and decide to bring children into the world we can never fully understand the new pressures we are bringing into our lives. But getting it right so that we launch happy and adjusted adults into the world takes patience, practice and time. As I said, parenting isn't always about getting it right and from time to time you will get it wrong. I know I do. Hopefully this book will have given you some practical advice to help you on this wonderful journey. Now all you have to do is buckle up!